Computer Hardware Course Study Book

Course Details:

This advance gives an outright outline of PC accessories parts, their capabilities, and interconnections. Understudies will accumulation involved associate with gathering, investigating, and headway PC frameworks.

Week 1-2: Introduction to Computer Hardware

1. Introduction to Computer Hardware

1. History and Evolution

2. Basic Components Overview

2. Computer Classification

1. Personal Computers (Desktop, Laptop, Workstation)
2. Servers
3. Embedded Systems

3. Understanding Motherboards

1. Form Factors
2. Chipset and Slots

4. Basic Input/Output Systems (BIOS)

1. Role and Function
2. BIOS Setup Utility

Week 3-4: Central Processing Unit (CPU)

1. CPU Architecture

1. CPU Components and Functions
2. Multi-core and Multi-threading

2. CPU Cooling and Thermal Management

1. Heat Sinks and Fans

2. Thermal Paste Application

3. Overclocking Basics

1. Risks and Rewards
2. Practical Overclocking Techniques

Week 5-6: Memory and Storage

1. Types of Memory

1. RAM (DDR, SRAM, DRAM)
2. ROM

2. Storage Devices

1. HDDs, SSDs, and Hybrid Drives
2. RAID Configurations

3. Storage Interfaces

1. SATA, NVMe, and more
2. External Storage Solutions

Week 7-8: Input and Output Devices

1. Keyboards and Mice

1. Mechanical vs. Membrane Keyboards
2. Gaming Mice and DPI

2. Monitors and Displays

1. Display Types (LED, LCD, OLED)
2. Refresh Rates and Resolution

3. Audio Devices

1. Sound Cards
2. Headphones, Speakers, and Microphones

Week 9-10: Expansion Cards and Connectivity

1. Graphics Cards (GPU)

1. GPU Architecture
2. SLI and CrossFire Technologies

2. Network Cards and Connectivity

1. Wired vs. Wireless Networking
2. Router and Switch Basics

3. Peripheral Connectivity

1. USB, Thunderbolt, and HDMI
2. Device Drivers and Installation

Week 11-12: Power Supplies and Cases

1. Understanding Power Supplies

1. Wattage and Efficiency
2. Modular vs. Non-modular PSUs

2. Computer Cases

1. Types and Form Factors
2. Cable Management

3. Cooling Systems

1. Case Fans and Airflow
2. Liquid Cooling Solutions

Week 13-14: Troubleshooting and Maintenance

1. Basic Troubleshooting Techniques

1. Common Issues and Solutions
2. Diagnostic Tools and Software

2. Software and Firmware Updates

1. Importance and Process
2. BIOS and Driver Updates

3. Preventative Maintenance

1. Cleaning and Dust Removal
2. Component Lifespan and Upgrades

Week 15-16: Advanced Topics and Emerging Trends

1. Emerging Hardware Technologies

1. Quantum Computing
2. Neuromorphic Hardware

2. Green Computing

1. Energy-efficient Hardware
2. E-waste Management

3. Hands-on Project

1. Build and Configure a Computer System
2. Troubleshoot and Optimize Performance

Assessment and Evaluation:

1. Weekly Quizzes and Assignments

2. Midterm Examination (covering Weeks 1-8)

3. Final Project and Presentation (covering Weeks 9-16)

Introduction to Computer Hardware

Definition: Computer hardware refers to the tangible components of a computer system that you can touch, see, and interact with physically. These components work together to process data and run software.

Basic Components Overview:

 **Central Processing Unit (CPU):** What it is: Often called the "brain" of the computer, the CPU executes instructions from software programs. Common Terminology: Cores, Clock Speed, Cache.

Memory (RAM): What it is: Temporary storage where the computer keeps data it's currently using.

Function: Allows for quick access and retrieval of data.

Storage:

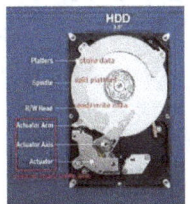

Hard Disk Drive (HDD): Traditional storage with spinning disks.

Solid State Drive (SSD): Faster storage without moving parts.

Purpose: Stores your files, software, and the operating system.

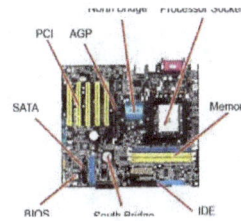

Motherboard:

What it is: Main circuit board connecting all other components.

Function: Provides pathways for data and power distribution.

Power Supply Unit (PSU): What it is: Provides electrical power to the computer.

Function: Converts electrical current from a wall outlet to the appropriate voltage for computer components.

Input and Output Devices:

Examples: Keyboard, mouse, monitor, printer.

Function: Allow users to input commands and receive information from the computer.

How They Work Together:

Imagine a computer as a busy office. The CPU is like the manager, the memory is the desk space where the current tasks are kept, and the storage is like the filing cabinets where all past work is stored. The motherboard acts as the office floor plan, connecting everything. Input devices are the tools (like pens and papers) employees use, and output devices are how they get feedback (like reading emails or seeing printed documents).

Importance:

Understanding computer hardware is essential for anyone using a computer, from casual users to IT professionals. Knowing the basics helps in making informed decisions about upgrades, troubleshooting problems, and optimizing performance.

History and Evolution of Computers

Origins:

1. Abacus (3000 BC): The abacus is one of the earliest known calculating tools, a manual device used for arithmetic calculations. It consists of beads or stones that can slide along rods or grooves.

Significance: One of the earliest tools for mathematical calculations.

2. Mechanical Calculators (1600s-1800s): Mechanical calculators are early devices designed to perform arithmetic operations. Before the advent of electronic calculators and computers, these machines represented the pinnacle of mechanical engineering and provided efficient means for numerical computations.

Significance: Reduced human error in calculations.

3. Early Computing Machines: Early computing machines are mechanical or electromechanical devices designed to perform specific tasks related to arithmetic calculations or data processing. Before the advent of electronic computers, these machines marked significant advancements in computational capabilities.

Charles Babbage: Analytical Engine 1837

1. Analytical Engine (1837): The Analytical Engine, conceived by Charles Babbage, is considered a pioneering design for a general-purpose mechanical computer. Although it was never fully constructed during Babbage's lifetime, its conceptual framework laid the foundation for modern computing principles.

Significance: Laid the foundation for modern computing principles.

2. Tabulating Machines (Late 1800s): Tabulating machines, notably developed by Herman Hollerith, were early electromechanical devices designed to process and analyze data using punched cards. These machines played a crucial role in automating data processing tasks, particularly for large-scale operations like census tabulations.

ENIAC (1945): ENIAC, which stands for Electronic Numerical Integrator and Computer, was one of the world's first general-purpose electronic digital computers. Developed during World War II at the University of Pennsylvania, ENIAC marked a significant advancement in computing technology, pioneering the transition from electromechanical to electronic computing systems.

Significance: Marked the beginning of electronic digital computing.

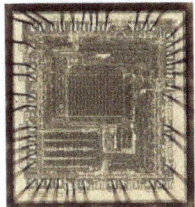

Transistors (1950s): Transistors are semiconductor devices that revolutionized electronics and computing in the 20th century. Invented in the 1940s and widely commercialized in the 1950s, transistors replaced bulky and less efficient vacuum tubes, leading to the development of smaller, faster, and more reliable electronic devices.

Significance: Made computers smaller, faster, and more efficient.

Microprocessors (1970s): A microprocessor is a central processing unit (CPU) contained on a single integrated circuit (IC) or chip. Emerging in the 1970s, microprocessors revolutionized computing by enabling the development of compact, affordable, and versatile computer systems.

Significance: Enabled the development of personal computers (PCs).

Rise of Personal Computers: The rise of personal computers (PCs) during the late 20th century transformed the computing landscape, making computing accessible to individuals and revolutionizing the way people work, communicate, and interact with technology.

Apple I (1976): The Apple I, introduced by Steve Wozniak and Steve Jobs in 1976, was Apple's first product and one of the earliest personal computers available as a pre-assembled motherboard. Sold as a kit, the Apple I played a pivotal role in the development of the personal computer industry.

Significance: Popularized the concept of home computing.

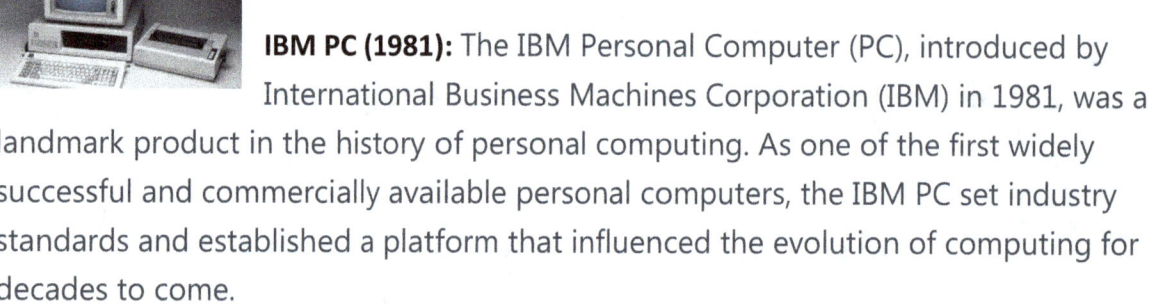

IBM PC (1981): The IBM Personal Computer (PC), introduced by International Business Machines Corporation (IBM) in 1981, was a landmark product in the history of personal computing. As one of the first widely successful and commercially available personal computers, the IBM PC set industry standards and established a platform that influenced the evolution of computing for decades to come.

Significance: Set the standard for PC hardware and software compatibility.

Modern Era and Beyond: The modern era of computing, spanning from the late 20th century to the present day, has witnessed unprecedented advancements and transformations, driven by rapid technological innovation, globalization, and the proliferation of digital technologies across various facets of society.

Laptops and Mobile Devices (1990s-2000s): The 1990s and 2000s witnessed the rapid development and proliferation of laptops and mobile devices, transforming computing and communication by enabling portable, convenient, and connected experiences for users around the world.

Significance: Revolutionized work and communication, making computing ubiquitous.

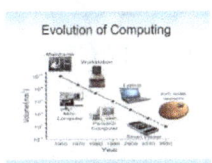

Cloud Computing (2010s): The 2010s witnessed the rapid growth and adoption of cloud computing, a paradigm shift in the delivery and consumption of computing resources and services, enabling organizations and individuals to access, store, and manage data and applications in a scalable and flexible manner via the internet.

Significance: Provides scalable and on-demand computing resources.

In Conclusion:

From simple counting tools to powerful supercomputers and cloud networks, the history of computers showcases humanity's relentless pursuit of innovation and efficiency. Each advancement has built upon the last, shaping the digital age we live in today.

<u>Computer Classification</u>

Computers can be classified into various categories based on their size, functionality, performance, and application. Understanding the different classifications helps in identifying the appropriate computer systems for specific tasks and requirements.

Supercomputers: Supercomputers are high-performance computing systems designed for executing complex and intensive computations, such as weather forecasting, scientific simulations, and advanced research applications.

Features: Exceptional processing speed, vast computational capabilities, and specialized architecture optimized for parallel processing.

MainFrame Computer

Mainframe Computers: Mainframe computers are robust and reliable computing systems typically used by large organizations and enterprises for critical business applications, such as transaction processing, data management, and centralized computing tasks.

Features: High processing power, extensive memory and storage capacities, and support for multiple concurrent users and applications.

Minicomputers (Midrange Computers): Minicomputers, also known as midrange computers, are computing systems that offer a balance between performance and affordability, suitable for medium-scale business operations and specific computing tasks.

Features: Moderate processing capabilities, scalable architecture, and support for networked environments and peripheral devices.

Type of Micro Computer

Microcomputers (Personal Computers): Microcomputers, commonly referred to as personal computers (PCs), are compact and affordable computing systems designed for individual use, productivity tasks, and general computing applications.

Features: Standard processing capabilities, diverse form factors (e.g., desktops, laptops, tablets), and support for a wide range of software and peripheral devices.

Workstations: Workstations are specialized computing systems optimized for high-performance graphics, engineering, and scientific applications, offering enhanced processing power and graphics capabilities compared to standard personal computers.

Features: Advanced processing and graphics capabilities, specialized hardware configurations, and support for professional software applications.

Examples of Embedded Computers

Embedded Computers: Embedded computers are computing systems integrated into other devices and systems to perform specific functions, such as control systems, consumer electronics, automotive applications, and IoT (Internet of Things) devices.

Features: Compact and energy-efficient design, tailored for specific applications and environments, and often operating in real-time or constrained computing environments.

Conclusion:

Computer classification provides a structured framework for understanding the diverse range of computing systems available today, each tailored to meet specific requirements, performance demands, and application scenarios. By categorizing computers based on their characteristics and capabilities, individuals and organizations can make informed decisions when selecting and deploying computing solutions that align with their needs and objectives.

Servers: A server is a specialized computer system designed to provide resources, services, and functionalities to other computers, devices, or users within a network environment. Servers play a crucial role in facilitating communication, data storage, processing, and collaboration across various computing environments.

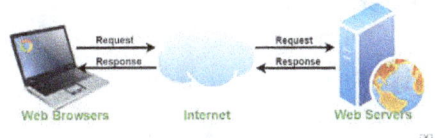

Web Servers: Web servers host websites, web applications, and web services, delivering content and services to users via the internet or intranet.

Features: HTTP (HyperText Transfer Protocol) support, web application hosting, content delivery, and security features like SSL/TLS encryption.

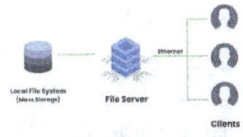

File Servers: File servers store, manage, and share files and data within a network, providing centralized access and collaboration capabilities for users and devices.

Features: File storage and management, user access control, file sharing protocols (e.g., SMB, NFS), and data backup and recovery.

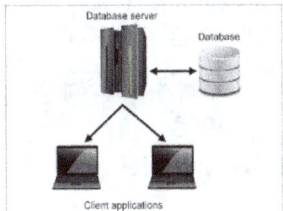

Database Servers: Database servers manage and store structured data, providing database management system (DBMS) functionalities for data organization, retrieval, and manipulation.

Features: Database management, data storage and indexing, query processing, transaction management, and data security and integrity.

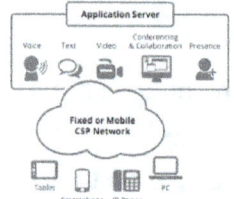

Application Servers: Application servers host and execute applications, providing runtime environments and services for application deployment, execution, and integration.

Features: Application hosting, middleware services, application deployment and management, integration capabilities, and support for various programming languages and frameworks.

Mail Servers: Mail servers handle email communication and messaging services, facilitating the exchange, storage, and retrieval of email messages between users and mail clients.

Features: Email routing and delivery, message storage and retrieval, user authentication and access control, and support for email protocols (e.g., SMTP, IMAP, POP3).

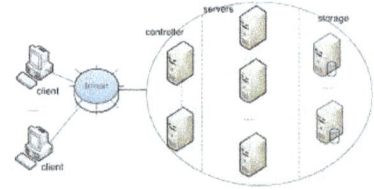

Virtual Servers (Virtual Machines): Virtual servers, or virtual machines (VMs), are software-based server instances created and managed within a virtualized environment, enabling multiple virtualized servers to run on a single physical server hardware.

Features: Virtualization technology, resource allocation and management, isolation and security, and flexibility in server deployment and scaling.

Conclusion:

Servers are integral components of modern computing environments, providing essential infrastructure and services that enable communication, collaboration, data management, and application execution across networks and systems. By understanding the different types and functionalities of servers, organizations can optimize their infrastructure, enhance performance, and meet the diverse computing needs and requirements of today's digital landscape.

Understanding Motherboards

A motherboard, also known as a main board or system board, is a crucial component of a computer system, serving as the central hub that connects and facilitates communication between various hardware components. Understanding the role, components, and features of a motherboard is essential for grasping the fundamentals of computer architecture and system integration.

Key Components of a Motherboard:

CPU Socket: The CPU (Central Processing Unit) socket is a specialized connector on the motherboard where the processor is installed, facilitating the interface between the CPU and the motherboard.

RAM Slots: RAM (Random Access Memory) slots are connectors on the motherboard for installing memory modules (RAM), providing temporary storage and fast access to data and instructions for the CPU.

Expansion Slots: Expansion slots, such as PCI (Peripheral Component Interconnect) and PCIe (PCI Express), allow for the installation of additional expansion cards, such as graphics cards, sound cards, and network adapters, to enhance system capabilities and functionality.

Storage Interfaces: Storage interfaces, including SATA (Serial ATA) and M.2 connectors, enable the connection and integration of storage devices, such as hard disk drives (HDDs) and solid-state drives (SSDs), for data storage and retrieval.

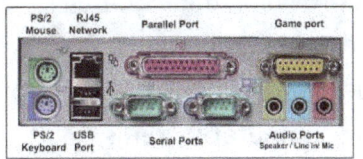

Connectors and Ports: Motherboards feature various connectors and ports, such as USB (Universal Serial Bus), HDMI, audio jacks, and networking ports, for connecting external devices, peripherals, and interfaces to the computer system.

Form Factors and Sizes:

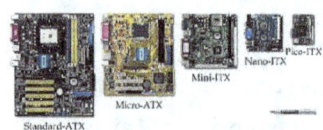

ATX: ATX (Advanced Technology eXtended) is a standard form factor for motherboards, defining the layout, dimensions, and mounting points, commonly used in desktop and workstation systems.

Micro-ATX and Mini-ITX: Micro-ATX and Mini-ITX are smaller form factors designed for compact and space-constrained systems, offering reduced size and layout variations to accommodate different chassis and system designs.

Server and Workstation Form Factors: Motherboards for server and workstation systems often adhere to specific form factors, such as EATX (Extended ATX), designed to meet the requirements of high-performance computing, scalability, and specialized configurations.

BIOS/UEFI and Firmware:

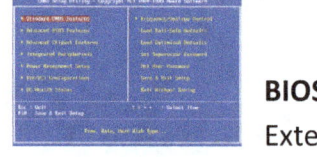

BIOS/UEFI: The BIOS (Basic Input/Output System) or UEFI (Unified Extensible Firmware Interface) is firmware embedded on the motherboard that initializes and configures system hardware, provides system services, and facilitates the boot process to load the operating system.

Firmware Updates: Firmware updates for the BIOS/UEFI are periodically released by motherboard manufacturers to enhance compatibility, performance, security, and functionality, requiring careful installation and configuration to ensure system stability and integrity.

Conclusion:

A motherboard is a foundational component of a computer system, providing the essential infrastructure and connectivity for integrating and coordinating hardware components. By understanding the components, features, and form factors of motherboards, individuals can make informed decisions when selecting, configuring, and upgrading computer systems, ensuring compatibility, performance, and functionality across diverse computing environments and applications.

Chipset and Slots

The chipset and slots on a motherboard play pivotal roles in facilitating communication between various hardware components and providing expansion capabilities for enhancing system functionality. Understanding the chipset architecture and slot configurations is essential for optimizing system performance, compatibility, and connectivity.

Chipset: The chipset is a set of integrated circuits (ICs) on the motherboard responsible for controlling and managing data flow between the CPU, memory, peripherals, and other system components.

Functionality: The chipset coordinates the interaction between the CPU and peripherals, manages system resources, controls data pathways, and provides interfaces for connecting external devices and expansion slots.

Types of Chipsets:

Northbridge: Traditionally responsible for connecting the CPU to high-speed components, such as RAM and graphics cards.

Southbridge: Manages lower-speed peripherals, including storage devices, USB ports, audio interfaces, and networking components.

Expansion Slots: Expansion slots are connectors on the motherboard designed to accommodate expansion cards, allowing users to add additional functionality and features to their computer systems.

Types of Expansion Slots:

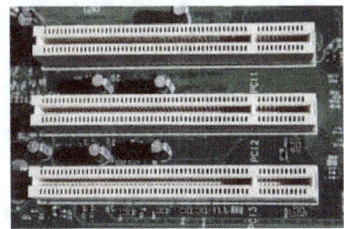

PCI (Peripheral Component Interconnect): A standard slot for connecting a variety of expansion cards, including sound cards, network adapters, and additional USB controllers.

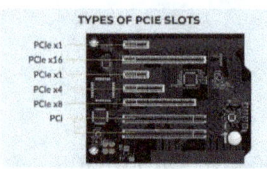

PCIe (PCI Express): A high-speed serial expansion bus offering increased bandwidth and scalability, commonly used for graphics cards, SSDs, network cards, and other high-performance peripherals.

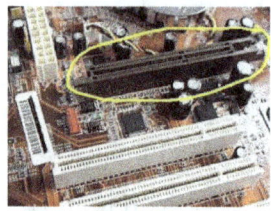

AGP (Accelerated Graphics Port): An older slot primarily used for connecting graphics cards, offering enhanced performance and capabilities compared to standard PCI slots (Note: Less relevant in modern systems).

Functionality: Expansion slots enable users to customize and upgrade their systems by adding specialized hardware components, such as graphics cards, sound cards, storage controllers, and networking adapters, to meet specific requirements and performance demands.

Conclusion:

The chipset and slots on a motherboard are integral components that contribute to the functionality, performance, and versatility of a computer system. By understanding the roles and capabilities of the chipset and expansion slots, individuals can make informed decisions when configuring, upgrading, or troubleshooting their systems, ensuring optimal compatibility, connectivity, and functionality across diverse computing environments and applications.

Basic Input/Output Systems (BIOS)

The Basic Input/Output System (BIOS) is firmware embedded on the motherboard of a computer system, serving as the fundamental interface between the hardware components and the operating system. BIOS initializes and configures system hardware during the boot process, facilitates communication between the hardware and software, and provides essential system services for managing and operating the computer system.

Role Functions of BIOS:

Hardware Initialization:

BIOS performs the initial power-on self-test (POST) to detect and initialize essential hardware components, including the CPU, RAM, storage devices, and peripherals, ensuring the system is ready for operation.

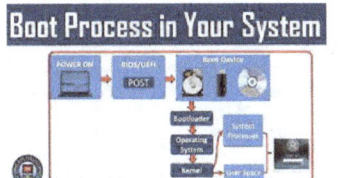

System Configuration:

BIOS provides a user interface (UEFI/BIOS setup) for configuring system settings, adjusting hardware parameters, enabling or disabling features, and managing system resources to optimize performance and compatibility.

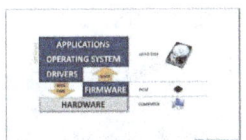

Boot Process Management:

BIOS initiates the boot process by loading the operating system from the designated boot device (e.g., hard drive, SSD, USB drive) into memory, executing the bootloader, and transferring control to the operating system to start the system initialization and user interface.

Driver and Firmware Execution:

BIOS executes and initializes firmware and drivers for essential system components and peripherals, enabling communication and interaction between the hardware components, operating system, and applications.

BIOS Components and Structure:

CMOS Memory:

The CMOS (Complementary Metal-Oxide-Semiconductor) memory stores BIOS settings, configuration parameters, system date and time, and hardware information, preserving settings across power cycles and reboots.

BIOS Chips:

BIOS is stored on non-volatile memory chips (e.g., ROM, EEPROM) on the motherboard, ensuring the firmware remains intact and accessible even when the system is powered off.

UEFI (Unified Extensible Firmware Interface):

UEFI is a modern firmware interface replacing traditional BIOS, offering enhanced features, compatibility, security, and performance optimizations, including support for larger storage devices (e.g., >2TB), faster boot times, and advanced configuration capabilities.

BIOS Updates and Maintenance:

Firmware Updates:

BIOS updates (or UEFI updates) are periodically released by motherboard manufacturers to provide enhancements, compatibility improvements, security patches, and support for new hardware components and technologies.

BIOS Recovery and Backup:

BIOS recovery mechanisms and backup utilities enable users to restore or update the firmware in case of corruption, compatibility issues, or unsuccessful update attempts, ensuring system reliability and integrity.

Conclusion:

The Basic Input/Output System (BIOS) is a critical component of computer systems, providing essential functions and services that enable hardware initialization, system configuration, and operating system booting. As technology evolves, the transition to UEFI and advancements in firmware management and security continue to shape the role and capabilities of BIOS in modern computing environments, emphasizing the importance of firmware maintenance, updates, and adherence to best practices for ensuring system compatibility, stability, and performance.

BIOS Setup Utility

The BIOS Setup Utility, often referred to as the BIOS settings or BIOS configuration, is an interface provided by the Basic Input/Output System (BIOS) firmware on a computer's motherboard. The BIOS Setup Utility allows users to view, modify, and manage system hardware settings and configurations, enabling customization, optimization, and troubleshooting of the computer system.

Accessing the BIOS Setup Utility:

Startup Sequence:

To access the BIOS Setup Utility, users typically press a specific key (e.g., F2, Del, F10, Esc) during the system boot-up process, before the operating system starts loading, to enter the BIOS interface.

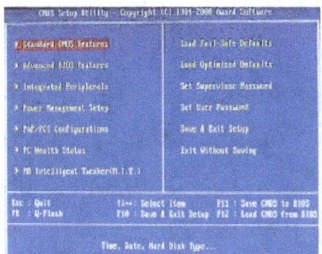

UEFI Firmware:

In modern systems with UEFI (Unified Extensible Firmware Interface), the BIOS Setup Utility may be accessed through UEFI settings, providing an enhanced and user-friendly interface for system configuration and management.

Key Features and Functions:

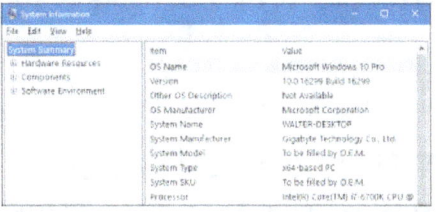

System Information:

The BIOS Setup Utility displays essential system information, including the BIOS version, motherboard model, CPU details, installed memory (RAM), and other hardware components, providing an overview of the system configuration.

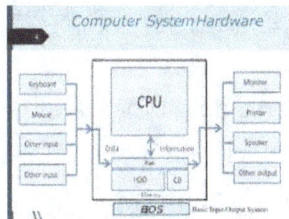

Hardware Configuration:

Users can configure various hardware settings and parameters, such as CPU settings, RAM timings, storage configurations, boot order, integrated peripherals (e.g., USB, SATA, audio), and power management options, to optimize performance and compatibility.

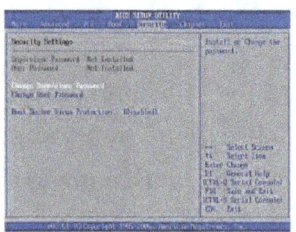

Security Settings:

The BIOS Setup Utility offers security settings to manage system security features, including password protection, secure boot, TPM (Trusted Platform Module) configuration, and other security-related options to enhance system integrity and data protection.

Advanced Settings:

Advanced settings in the BIOS Setup Utility provide additional customization and control over system functionalities, offering options for hardware monitoring, overclocking (if supported), virtualization, chipset settings, and other advanced configurations to meet specific requirements and preferences.

Save and Exit:

After configuring the desired settings in the BIOS Setup Utility, users can save the changes and exit the interface, triggering a system reboot to apply the new configurations and ensure proper operation with the updated settings.

Conclusion:

The BIOS Setup Utility is a critical tool for managing and configuring system hardware settings and parameters, enabling users to customize and optimize their computer systems according to their requirements and preferences. By accessing and utilizing the BIOS Setup Utility effectively, users can enhance system performance, ensure compatibility, implement security measures, and troubleshoot hardware-related issues to maintain and optimize the functionality and reliability of their computer systems.

Central Processing Unit (CPU)

The Central Processing Unit (CPU) is often referred to as the "brain" of a computer, responsible for executing instructions, performing calculations, and coordinating the operation of hardware components to process data and execute tasks. Understanding the CPU's role, architecture, and characteristics is essential for grasping the fundamental principles of computer operation and performance.

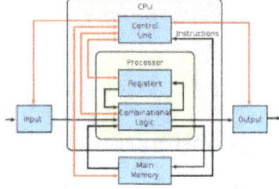

CPU Architecture

ISA defines the set of instructions, operations, data types, and addressing modes supported by the CPU, specifying the interface and functionality that software applications and operating systems can utilize to interact with the CPU and execute tasks.

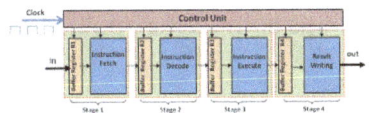

CPU Pipeline Architecture:

Instruction Pipeline:

The CPU employs a pipeline architecture to enhance processing efficiency by dividing the instruction execution process into stages (e.g., fetch, decode, execute, writeback), allowing multiple instructions to be processed concurrently and overlapping the execution of successive instructions to maximize throughput and performance.

Pipeline Stages:

The pipeline stages represent the sequential phases of the instruction execution process within the CPU, each stage performing specific tasks and operations to progress the instruction through the pipeline and contribute to the overall processing speed and efficiency of the CPU.

CPU Types and Architectures:

CISC (Complex Instruction Set Computer):

CISC architecture supports a rich set of complex instructions, enabling high-level operations to be performed with a single instruction, but potentially leading to increased complexity, power consumption, and variability in instruction execution times.

RISC (Reduced Instruction Set Computer):

RISC architecture focuses on a simplified instruction set, promoting the use of fundamental instructions and efficient execution techniques to optimize performance, reduce hardware complexity, and enhance scalability and power efficiency.

Multi-core and Parallel Architectures:

Modern CPUs employ multi-core and parallel architectures, integrating multiple processing cores and leveraging parallel processing techniques to enhance performance, concurrency, and multitasking capabilities by executing multiple threads and tasks concurrently across the CPU cores.

Conclusion:

CPU architecture encompasses the design, organization, and functionality of the Central Processing Unit, defining the internal components, instruction execution process, and architectural characteristics that shape the performance, efficiency, and capabilities of the CPU. By understanding CPU architecture, individuals can appreciate the principles of hardware design, optimization techniques, and the impact of architectural choices on

CPU performance, compatibility, and suitability for various computing applications and requirements.

CPU Cooling and Thermal Management

CPU cooling and thermal management are critical aspects of computer hardware design, ensuring that the Central Processing Unit (CPU) operates within safe temperature limits. Efficient cooling is essential to prevent overheating, maintain system stability, and optimize the performance and longevity of the CPU.

Heat Sinks and Fans

Heat Generation:

During operation, a CPU generates heat due to the electrical resistance in its components and the energy consumed during the execution of tasks. Excessive heat can lead to performance degradation and potential damage to the CPU.

Temperature Limits:

CPUs have specified temperature limits beyond which they may experience thermal throttling (reducing performance to prevent overheating) or shut down to prevent damage. Effective cooling ensures that the CPU operates within these limits.

Cooling Methods:

Air Cooling:

Heat Sink: A heat sink is a passive cooling device with fins that dissipate heat from the CPU. A fan, often attached to the heat sink, enhances heat dissipation by increasing airflow.

CPU Fan: Dedicated fans, commonly known as CPU fans, direct airflow over the heat sink to cool the CPU. Air coolers are popular for their simplicity, affordability, and reliability.

Liquid Cooling:

Liquid Cooler: Liquid cooling systems use a closed loop with a pump, radiator, and liquid-filled tubes. The liquid absorbs heat from the CPU and transfers it to the radiator, where a fan dissipates the heat.

AIO (All-in-One): AIO liquid coolers come pre-assembled, making them easier to install compared to custom liquid cooling setups. They provide efficient cooling with a reduced risk of leaks.

Thermal Paste Application

Thermal Paste:

Thermal paste is applied between the CPU and the heat sink to enhance thermal conductivity and fill microscopic gaps, ensuring better heat transfer. Proper application of thermal paste is crucial for effective cooling.

Factors Affecting Cooling Performance:

Cooler Design and Size:

The design and size of the cooler, including the heat sink and fan, influence its ability to dissipate heat effectively. Larger heat sinks and fans generally provide better cooling.

Airflow in the Chassis:

Adequate airflow within the computer case helps carry heat away from components. Proper cable management, case fan placement, and clean air filters contribute to optimal airflow.

Ambient Temperature:

The ambient temperature of the room or environment affects the cooling efficiency. Higher ambient temperatures can reduce the overall effectiveness of cooling solutions.

Thermal Management Features:

Temperature Monitoring:

Motherboards often include temperature sensors that monitor CPU temperatures. Users can check these values through BIOS/UEFI or monitoring software.

Fan Speed Control:

Motherboards or dedicated fan controllers can adjust fan speeds based on temperature. This feature helps balance cooling performance and noise levels.

Thermal Throttling:

CPUs may employ thermal throttling to reduce their clock speeds when temperatures become too high. This protective measure prevents overheating and potential damage.

Conclusion:

CPU cooling and thermal management are integral components of computer system design, ensuring reliable and efficient operation. Proper cooling solutions, whether air or liquid, along with thoughtful thermal management practices, contribute to system stability, performance, and the overall lifespan of the CPU.

Overclocking Basics

1. Risks and Rewards:

Risks:

Heat Generation: Overclocking increases the workload on the CPU, generating more heat. If not managed properly, this can lead to overheating, affecting stability and potentially damaging the CPU.

Component Wear: Over time, overclocking may contribute to increased wear on CPU components. Excessive overclocking without adequate cooling can accelerate this wear and reduce the lifespan of the CPU.

Data Corruption: Unstable overclocks may cause system crashes or data corruption. It's crucial to find a stable overclock to avoid potential data loss or system instability.

Rewards:

Performance Boost: Overclocking can provide a noticeable performance boost, especially in tasks that are CPU-intensive. This can lead to faster rendering times, improved gaming performance, and overall responsiveness.

Cost-Efficiency: Instead of immediately upgrading to a more powerful CPU, overclocking allows users to maximize the potential of their existing hardware, delaying the need for an upgrade.

Personalization: Overclocking allows users to tailor their system's performance to their specific needs, balancing power and efficiency based on individual preferences.

2. Practical Overclocking Techniques:

a. Stress Testing and Monitoring:

Stress Testing: Before overclocking, stress test the CPU to identify its baseline performance and thermal characteristics. Tools like Prime95 and AIDA64 can help stress test the CPU.

Temperature Monitoring: Use temperature monitoring tools to keep track of the CPU temperature during stress tests and regular usage. Keeping temperatures within safe limits is crucial for stability.

b. BIOS/UEFI Settings:

Multiplier and Frequency: Adjust the CPU multiplier and base clock frequency in the BIOS/UEFI to increase the clock speed. However, be cautious as increasing these values can lead to instability.

Voltage Settings: Adjusting CPU voltage can help stabilize overclocks. However, excessive voltage increases can contribute to higher temperatures and reduce the CPU's lifespan.

c. Incremental Changes:

Gradual Overclocking: Incrementally increase clock speeds and voltages, testing stability after each change. This approach helps find the optimal balance between performance and stability.

Memory Overclocking: Overclocking RAM can complement CPU overclocking, enhancing overall system performance. Adjust memory timings and frequencies cautiously.

d. Cooling Solutions:

Quality Cooling: Invest in high-quality cooling solutions, such as aftermarket air coolers or liquid cooling systems. Effective cooling is crucial for managing increased heat generated by overclocking.

Thermal Paste: Apply quality thermal paste between the CPU and the cooler for improved heat transfer. Proper cooling ensures stable performance under overclocked conditions.

e. Backup and Restore:

BIOS/UEFI Profiles: Save multiple profiles in the BIOS/UEFI to easily switch between overclocked and default settings. This allows quick recovery in case of instability.

Backup System: Before overclocking, ensure important data is backed up. Overclocking carries a small risk of system instability, and having a backup is a precautionary measure.

Conclusion:
Overclocking, when done responsibly, can offer tangible benefits in terms of improved performance and personalized system optimization. However, it requires careful consideration of risks, meticulous testing, and adherence to safe practices to avoid potential downsides such as overheating and instability. Users should approach overclocking with caution, gradually experimenting with settings while monitoring temperatures and ensuring system stability.

Memory and Storage

Types of Memory

1. RAM (Random Access Memory):

a. DDR SDRAM (Double Data Rate Synchronous Dynamic RAM):
DDR SDRAM is a type of volatile memory commonly used in computers for temporary data storage. It is synchronized with the system clock and transfers data on both the rising and falling edges of the clock signal, providing higher bandwidth compared to its predecessor, SDR SDRAM.

Characteristics:

DDR, DDR2, DDR3, DDR4: Different generations with varying speeds and improvements in data transfer rates.

Faster Access Speed: DDR RAM offers faster read and write speeds compared to SDR RAM, enhancing overall system performance.

Widely Used: DDR SDRAM is the standard RAM type in modern computers and is used for tasks like running applications and multitasking.

b. SRAM (Static Random Access Memory):
SRAM is another type of volatile memory that differs from DRAM (Dynamic RAM) in that it uses latching circuitry to store each bit of data. This eliminates the need for constant refreshing, making SRAM faster but more expensive than DRAM.

Characteristics:

Faster Access Speed: SRAM provides faster access times than DRAM since it doesn't require periodic refreshing.

Higher Cost: SRAM is more expensive to manufacture than DRAM due to its more complex design and lower storage density.

Cache Memory: SRAM is often used as cache memory in CPUs for quick access to frequently used data.

c. DRAM (Dynamic Random Access Memory):
DRAM is a type of volatile memory that requires constant refreshing to retain data. It is widely used as the main

system memory in computers, providing a balance between cost, density, and performance.

Characteristics:

Lower Cost per Bit: DRAM is less expensive to manufacture compared to SRAM, making it suitable for high-capacity memory modules.

Slower Access Speed: DRAM has slower access times compared to SRAM due to the need for refreshing.

Main System Memory: DRAM modules are the primary memory used for storing data that the CPU needs during operation.

2. ROM (Read-Only Memory):

ROM is non-volatile memory used to store permanent data or firmware that should not be modified during normal operation. It retains its content even when the power is turned off.

Types of ROM:

Mask ROM: Permanent data is "masked" onto the chip during manufacturing and cannot be changed.

EPROM (Erasable Programmable Read-Only Memory): Can be erased and reprogrammed using ultraviolet light.

EEPROM (Electrically Memory): Can be

Erasable Programmable Read-Only electronically erased and reprogrammed.

Applications:

Boot Firmware: ROM stores the system's boot firmware, ensuring that essential instructions are always available during startup.

Embedded Systems: ROM is commonly used in embedded systems and devices where permanent data storage is required.

Conclusion:

Understanding the different types of memory, including RAM (DDR, SRAM, DRAM) and ROM, is crucial for comprehending their roles in computer systems. These memory types contribute to the overall functionality, performance, and data storage capabilities of electronic devices, each serving specific purposes in the execution of tasks and storage of essential firmware or permanent data.

Storage Devices

1. HDDs, SSDs, and Hybrid Drives:

 **a. HDD (Hard Disk Drive):** HDDs are traditional storage devices that use magnetic storage to store and retrieve data. They consist of spinning disks (platters) coated with a magnetic material, read/write heads, and a motor to spin the disks.

Capacity: HDDs are available in high capacities, making them suitable for storing large amounts of data.

Cost-Effective: HDDs are generally more cost-effective in terms of price per gigabyte compared to SSDs.

Mechanical Components: Due to moving parts (spinning disks and heads), HDDs are more susceptible to mechanical failure.

 **b. SSD (Solid State Drive):** SSDs use NAND-based flash memory for data storage. Unlike HDDs, SSDs have no moving parts, which provides several advantages in terms of speed, durability, and energy efficiency.

Speed: SSDs offer faster data access and transfer speeds compared to HDDs, leading to quicker system boot times and application loading.

Durability: With no moving parts, SSDs are more durable and less prone to physical damage caused by drops or shocks.

Energy Efficiency: SSDs consume less power than HDDs, contributing to improved energy efficiency in laptops and other portable devices.

 **c. Hybrid Drives (SSHD):** Hybrid drives combine elements of both HDDs and SSDs in a single device. They feature a traditional HDD with a smaller SSD cache, allowing for a balance between capacity and performance.

Improved Performance: Hybrid drives leverage the SSD cache to store frequently accessed data, enhancing overall performance without sacrificing storage capacity.

Cost-Effective: Compared to standalone SSDs, hybrid drives are more cost-effective while providing a performance boost over traditional HDDs.

Automatic Data Management: The drive's firmware automatically determines which data to store in the SSD cache based on usage patterns.

2. RAID Configurations:

a. RAID (Redundant Array of Independent Disks): RAID is a technology that involves combining multiple physical drives into a single logical unit to improve performance, redundancy, or a combination of both.

Common RAID Configurations:

RAID 0 (Striping):

Performance: Improves read and write speeds by striping data across multiple drives.

No Redundancy: Offers no data redundancy; the failure of one drive results in data loss.

RAID 1 (Mirroring):

Redundancy: Mirrors data across two drives, providing redundancy.

Performance Impact: Read performance is improved, but write performance may be slightly reduced.

RAID 5 (Striping with Parity):

Performance: Balances performance and redundancy by striping data and including parity information.

Fault Tolerance: Can withstand the failure of one drive without data loss.

RAID 10 (Striping and Mirroring):

Combination: Combines the benefits of both RAID 0 and RAID 1 by striping and mirroring.

Performance and Redundancy: Offers improved performance and redundancy but requires a larger number of drives.

Applications: RAID configurations are commonly used in servers and enterprise environments to enhance storage performance, availability, and reliability.

RAID can be implemented using hardware controllers or software-based solutions provided by the operating system.

Conclusion:

Understanding the characteristics and configurations of storage devices, including HDDs, SSDs, and hybrid drives, as well as RAID configurations, is essential for making informed decisions when selecting storage solutions based on performance, capacity, and redundancy requirements. Each type of storage device and RAID configuration serves specific needs, and the choice depends on factors such as speed, durability, capacity, and fault tolerance.

<h1 align="center">Storage Interfaces</h1>

<h2 align="center">1. SATA, NVMe, and More:</h2>

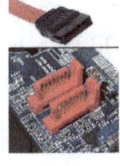

a. SATA (Serial ATA): SATA is a standard storage interface widely used for connecting internal storage devices such as hard disk drives (HDDs) and solid-state drives (SSDs) to a computer's motherboard.

Speed: SATA comes in different versions (e.g., SATA I, SATA II, SATA III), with SATA III being the most common, supporting data transfer speeds up to 6 gigabits per second (Gbps).

Compatibility: SATA is backward compatible, allowing newer drives to work with older SATA interfaces, but at the speed of the slower interface.

b. NVMe (Non-Volatile Memory Express): NVMe is a newer and faster storage interface designed specifically for flash-based storage devices like SSDs. It operates over the PCIe (Peripheral Component Interconnect Express) bus.

Speed: NVMe provides significantly higher data transfer speeds compared to SATA, with modern NVMe SSDs reaching speeds of several gigabytes per second.

Low Latency: NVMe reduces latency, enabling quicker access to data and improving overall system responsiveness.

M.2 Form Factor: NVMe SSDs often use the M.2 form factor, which is smaller and more compact than traditional SATA drives.

c. PCIe (Peripheral Component Interconnect Express): PCIe is a high-speed interface standard used for various components in a computer, including graphics cards, network cards, and storage devices (NVMe SSDs).

Speed: PCIe provides high-speed data transfer between the motherboard and connected devices, with multiple lanes (e.g., x1, x4, x8, x16) determining the bandwidth.

Scalability: PCIe allows for scalable bandwidth, accommodating the increasing demands of modern applications and devices.

Compatibility: PCIe slots are versatile and can support various expansion cards, making them widely used in modern computers.

d. USB (Universal Serial Bus): USB is a widely used standard for connecting external devices to computers. USB interfaces are commonly used for external storage solutions, including flash drives and external hard drives.

Versatility: USB interfaces come in different versions (e.g., USB 2.0, USB 3.0, USB 3.1, USB 3.2) with varying data transfer speeds and compatibility.

Plug-and-Play: USB is known for its plug-and-play functionality, allowing easy connection and disconnection of devices without restarting the computer.

Power Delivery: USB can provide power to connected devices, eliminating the need for additional power sources in some cases.

2. External Storage Solutions:

a. External Hard Drives: External hard drives are portable storage solutions that use traditional HDD technology and connect to computers via USB or other interfaces.

Large Capacities: External hard drives offer high-capacity storage options suitable for backup and large file storage.

Cost-Effective: External HDDs are generally more cost-effective than SSDs, providing ample storage at a reasonable price.

b. External SSDs: External SSDs utilize solid-state storage technology and connect to computers through interfaces like USB or Thunderbolt, providing faster data transfer speeds than external HDDs.

Speed: External SSDs offer faster data transfer speeds compared to external HDDs, resulting in quicker file transfers and improved performance.

Durability: SSDs have no moving parts, making external SSDs more resistant to physical shocks and vibrations.

c. USB Flash Drives: USB flash drives, also known as thumb drives or memory sticks, are compact, portable storage devices that connect to computers via USB ports.

Portability: USB flash drives are small and lightweight, making them highly portable and convenient for transferring files between devices.

Plug-and-Play: Flash drives are plug-and-play devices, requiring no additional power sources or complex setup.

Conclusion:

Understanding storage interfaces such as SATA, NVMe, PCIe, and USB, along with external storage solutions like external hard drives, external SSDs, and USB flash drives, is crucial for selecting the right storage solution based on performance, capacity, and portability requirements. Each storage interface and external storage type serves specific needs, offering a range of options for users seeking efficient and reliable data storage solutions.

Keyboards and Mice

1. Mechanical vs. Membrane Keyboards:

 **a. Mechanical Keyboards:** Mechanical keyboards use individual mechanical switches for each key. These switches have a distinct tactile feel and audible click, providing a responsive typing experience.

Tactile Feedback: Mechanical switches offer tactile feedback, allowing users to feel when a key has been actuated. This feature is beneficial for touch typists and gamers.

Durability: Mechanical keyboards are known for their durability, with switches rated for tens of millions of keystrokes.

Customization: Some mechanical keyboards allow users to customize the type of switches, choosing between linear, tactile, or clicky switches based on personal preferences.

 **b. Membrane Keyboards:** Membrane keyboards use a pressure pad or membrane to register key presses. The keys are generally quieter and have a softer feel compared to mechanical keyboards.

Quiet Operation: Membrane keyboards are quieter than their mechanical counterparts, making them suitable for shared or quiet environments.

Lower Cost: Membrane keyboards are often more affordable than mechanical keyboards, making them a budget-friendly option.

Smoother Keystrokes: The keys on a membrane keyboard typically have a smoother and softer feel compared to the tactile and clicky nature of mechanical switches.

Comparison:

Typing Experience: Mechanical keyboards are preferred by users who enjoy a tactile and audible typing experience, while membrane keyboards provide a quieter and softer typing experience.

Gaming: Mechanical keyboards are popular among gamers for their precise actuation and tactile feedback. Membrane keyboards can be suitable for casual gamers or those on a budget.

2. Gaming Mice and DPI:

 **a. Gaming Mice:** Gaming mice are designed with features that enhance gaming performance, including precision, speed, and customizable options.

High DPI: Gaming mice often have high DPI (Dots Per Inch) sensitivity, allowing for quick and precise cursor movements.

Programmable Buttons: Gaming mice may have extra programmable buttons that can be customized for in-game commands, providing quick access to specific functions.

Ergonomic Design: Many gaming mice feature ergonomic designs with comfortable grips to accommodate long gaming sessions.

b. DPI (Dots Per Inch): DPI is a measure of the sensitivity of a mouse. Higher DPI settings result in faster cursor movements across the screen.

Precision: Higher DPI settings provide greater precision in cursor movements, allowing for precise targeting in games.

Adjustability: Gaming mice often come with adjustable DPI settings, allowing users to switch between different sensitivity levels based on their preferences or specific in-game scenarios.

Customization: DPI settings can be customized using software that accompanies gaming mice, giving users control over their preferred sensitivity.

Comparison:

Gaming Performance: Gaming mice with higher DPI settings are favored by gamers who require precise and quick movements, especially in fast-paced games.

Regular Use: While gaming mice excel in gaming scenarios, they may also be used for regular computer tasks. Users can adjust DPI settings to suit their preferences for different applications.

Conclusion:

Choosing between mechanical and membrane keyboards, as well as understanding the importance of DPI in gaming mice, depends on individual preferences and use cases. Mechanical keyboards offer a tactile and customizable typing experience, while membrane keyboards provide a quieter and more budget-friendly option. Gaming mice, with their high DPI and customizable features, cater to the specific needs of gamers, providing precision and flexibility in various gaming scenarios.

Monitors and Displays
1. Display Types (LED, LCD, OLED):

a. LED (Light-Emitting Diode): LED displays use light-emitting diodes to provide backlighting for the screen. They are a common type of display technology used in various devices, including computer monitors and TVs.

Energy-Efficient: LED displays are energy-efficient compared to traditional backlighting methods.

Slim Design: LED technology allows for slim and lightweight display designs.

Brightness: LED displays can achieve high levels of brightness, contributing to vibrant and vivid visuals.

b. LCD (Liquid Crystal Display): LCD displays use liquid crystal technology to modulate light and create images. They often incorporate LED backlighting for illumination.
Color Accuracy: LCD displays offer good color accuracy and are suitable for various applications.
Affordability: LCD monitors are often more affordable than OLED displays.
Common Technology: LCD technology is widespread and commonly used in a range of devices.

 **c. OLED (Organic Light-Emitting Diode):** OLED displays use organic compounds that emit light when an electric current is applied. Each pixel is self-illuminating, allowing for deep blacks and vibrant colors.
Perfect Blacks: OLED displays can achieve true black levels since each pixel emits its own light.
Wide Viewing Angles: OLEDs offer wide viewing angles and consistent colors from various perspectives.
Thin and Flexible: OLED technology allows for thin and flexible display designs.
Comparison:
Contrast Ratio: OLEDs typically have a higher contrast ratio than LED and LCD displays, resulting in more vivid and lifelike images.
Durability: OLED displays may be susceptible to burn-in, where static images displayed for extended periods can cause permanent damage. LED and LCD displays are generally more resistant to burn-in.

2. Refresh Rates and Resolution:

a. Refresh Rates: Refresh rate refers to how many times per second the display refreshes the image. It is measured in Hertz (Hz).
Smooth Motion: Higher refresh rates, such as 60Hz, 120Hz, or 144Hz, result in smoother motion, reducing motion blur in fast-paced scenes.
Gaming Performance: Gamers often prefer monitors with higher refresh rates for more responsive gameplay.
Standard Refresh Rates: 60Hz is a standard refresh rate for most monitors, suitable for general computing tasks.
b. Resolution: Resolution refers to the number of pixels on the screen, typically expressed as the number of pixels horizontally by the number of pixels vertically (e.g., 1920x1080, commonly known as Full HD).
Image Clarity: Higher resolutions, such as 4K (3840x2160), provide sharper and clearer images.

Productivity: Higher resolutions offer more screen real estate, improving productivity for tasks such as video editing or multitasking.

Hardware Requirements: Higher resolutions may require more powerful graphics hardware to maintain smooth performance, especially in gaming.

Comparison:

Gaming vs. Productivity: While high refresh rates are crucial for gaming, high resolutions are beneficial for tasks that require detailed visuals, such as photo or video editing.

Balance: Monitors with a balance of both high refresh rates and resolutions are popular for users seeking an all-around display for gaming and productivity.

Conclusion:

Choosing the right display type, whether LED, LCD, or OLED, depends on factors like budget, preferences, and specific use cases. Understanding refresh rates and resolutions is crucial for tailoring the monitor to individual needs, whether for gaming, content creation, or general computing tasks. Each technology offers its unique advantages, allowing users to find the display that best suits their requirements.

Audio Devices

1. Sound Cards: Sound cards are hardware components responsible for processing and outputting audio signals. They can be integrated into the motherboard or added as dedicated expansion cards.

Audio Processing: Sound cards process digital audio signals into analog signals that can be played through speakers or headphones.

Connectivity: Sound cards provide various audio ports, including line-out for speakers, line-in for external audio sources, and headphone jacks.

Audio Quality: Dedicated sound cards often offer better audio quality and features compared to onboard audio solutions.

Types of Sound Cards:

Integrated Audio: Most motherboards come with integrated audio solutions, providing basic audio functionality suitable for everyday use.

Dedicated Sound Cards: Audiophiles and content creators may opt for dedicated sound cards with higher audio quality, additional features, and improved signal-to-noise ratios.

2. Headphones, Speakers, and Microphones:

a. Headphones: Headphones are audio devices worn on the head, covering the ears, and delivering audio directly to the listener.

Types: There are various types of headphones, including over-ear, on-ear, and in-ear, each offering different levels of comfort and sound isolation.

Impedance: Impedance measures the resistance to electrical current. Higher impedance headphones may require more powerful amplification for optimal performance.

 **b. Speakers:** Speakers convert electrical signals into sound waves, providing audio output for a broader audience.

Types: Speakers come in various types, including bookshelf, floor-standing, and surround sound speakers, each suitable for different setups.

Configuration: Speaker systems can be stereo (2.0), 2.1 (with a subwoofer), or multi-channel (5.1, 7.1) for immersive audio experiences.

c. Microphones: Microphones capture audio signals and convert them into electrical signals for recording or communication purposes.

Types: Microphones come in different types, including condenser and dynamic microphones, each suitable for specific applications.

Connection: Microphones may connect through USB or analog ports, and some are built into headphones for hands-free communication.

Directionality: Microphones can be omnidirectional, capturing sound from all directions, or directional, focusing on specific sound sources.

Additional Considerations:

Wireless vs. Wired: Headphones, speakers, and microphones may be available in both wired and wireless options, providing flexibility in usage.

Gaming Audio: Gaming-focused headphones often come with features like surround sound, spatial audio, and built-in microphones for immersive gaming experiences.

Conclusion:

Understanding the various components of audio devices, including sound cards, headphones, speakers, and microphones, allows users to tailor their audio setup to their specific needs. Whether for gaming, content creation, or everyday audio enjoyment, selecting the right combination of audio devices contributes to a satisfying and immersive audio experience.

Expansion Cards and Connectivity
Graphics Cards (GPU)

1. GPU Architecture: GPU (Graphics Processing Unit) architecture refers to the design and structure of the graphics card's processing components. Different GPU architectures offer varying levels of performance, features, and efficiency.

a. NVIDIA GPU Architectures:

Pascal (GTX 10 Series): Introduced in 2016, Pascal brought improvements in performance and power efficiency.

Features: GDDR5 and GDDR5X memory, simultaneous multi-projection, and improved VR capabilities.

Turing (GTX 16 Series, RTX 20 Series): Released in 2018, Turing introduced real-time ray tracing for more realistic lighting and reflections.

Features: Tensor cores for AI-based features, GDDR6 memory, and improved performance for gaming and content creation.

Ampere (RTX 30 Series): Introduced in 2020, Ampere focuses on increased CUDA cores and improved ray tracing performance.

Features: Second-generation RT cores, third-generation Tensor cores, and support for PCIe 4.0.

b. AMD GPU Architectures:

Graphics Core Next (GCN): GCN architecture, used in various AMD GPUs, aimed to deliver parallel processing power.

Features: Compute-oriented design, support for DirectX 12, and HBM (High Bandwidth Memory) support.

RDNA (Radeon DNA): RDNA, introduced in 2019, focuses on gaming performance and efficiency.

Features: Improved compute units, GDDR6 memory support, and optimized for gaming workloads.

RDNA 2: RDNA 2, featured in the RX 6000 Series, includes advancements in ray tracing and overall performance.

Features: Ray Accelerators for real-time ray tracing, Infinity Cache for improved memory bandwidth, and support for DirectX 12 Ultimate.

2. SLI and CrossFire Technologies: SLI (Scalable Link Interface) and CrossFire are technologies developed by NVIDIA and AMD, respectively, to allow multiple GPUs to work together for enhanced graphics performance.

a. SLI (NVIDIA):

Configuration: In SLI, two or more NVIDIA GPUs can be connected using an SLI bridge.

Performance: SLI is designed to improve gaming performance by distributing rendering tasks among multiple GPUs.

Compatibility: Not all games and applications are optimized for SLI, and scaling may vary depending on the software.

b. CrossFire (AMD):

Configuration: CrossFire allows two or more AMD GPUs to work in tandem to improve graphics performance.

Performance: Similar to SLI, CrossFire aims to enhance gaming performance by dividing rendering tasks.

Compatibility: Game and application support for CrossFire may vary, and not all software is optimized for multi-GPU configurations.

Considerations:

Diminishing Returns: While SLI and CrossFire can offer increased performance, the scaling is not always linear, and the performance gains may not justify the cost of an additional GPU.

Game Support: The effectiveness of SLI and CrossFire depends on how well games and applications support multi-GPU configurations. Some newer titles may not optimize for these technologies.

Conclusion:

Understanding GPU architectures, such as NVIDIA's Pascal, Turing, and Ampere, or AMD's GCN, RDNA, and RDNA 2, allows users to make informed decisions based on their performance and feature requirements. Additionally, awareness of SLI and CrossFire technologies provides insights into the potential for leveraging multiple GPUs to enhance graphics performance, although careful consideration is necessary due to diminishing returns and varying game support.

Network Cards and Connectivity
1. Wired vs. Wireless Networking:

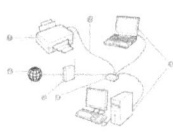

a. Wired Networking: Wired networking uses physical cables (such as Ethernet cables) to connect devices within a network.

Reliability: Wired connections are generally more reliable than wireless, offering consistent and stable data transfer.

Speed: Wired connections can provide higher data transfer speeds compared to wireless, making them suitable for bandwidth-intensive tasks.

Security: Wired networks are often considered more secure because they are harder to intercept compared to wireless signals.

 **b. Wireless Networking:** Wireless networking utilizes radio waves to connect devices without the need for physical cables.

Convenience: Wireless networks provide flexibility and convenience, allowing devices to connect without physical constraints.

Mobility: Devices can move freely within the wireless network's range, making it ideal for mobile devices like laptops and smartphones.

Installation: Setting up a wireless network is generally easier than installing wired connections, especially in situations where wiring is impractical.

Comparison:

Use Case: Wired connections are often preferred for desktop computers, gaming consoles, and devices that require high-speed and reliable connections. Wireless is suitable for portable devices and areas where running cables is challenging.

Speed: In general, wired connections offer higher speeds and lower latency compared to wireless, making them preferable for tasks like online gaming or large file transfers.

2. Router and Switch Basics:

 **a. Router:** A router is a networking device that connects different networks together, such as a local network and the internet.

Functions:

Network Address Translation (NAT): Routers use NAT to manage the translation of private IP addresses within a local network to a single public IP address for internet communication.

Routing: Routers direct data packets between devices within the local network and external networks like the internet.

Firewall: Many routers include a built-in firewall to enhance network security.

b. Switch: A switch is a device that connects multiple devices within a local network, allowing them to communicate with each other.

Functions:

Local Connectivity: Switches create a network within a specific location (e.g., a home or office) by connecting multiple devices like computers, printers, and other networked devices.

Data Forwarding: Switches forward data only to the device for which the data is intended, reducing network congestion and improving efficiency.

Port Management: Managed switches offer features like VLANs (Virtual Local Area Networks) for segmenting networks and improving security.

Comparison:

Role in the Network: Routers manage traffic between different networks, while switches facilitate communication within a local network.

Functionality: A router often includes a built-in switch, allowing it to connect multiple devices within a local network. However, switches focus on local connectivity.

Conclusion:

Understanding the differences between wired and wireless networking, as well as the basic functions of routers and switches, is crucial for setting up and maintaining effective and reliable network connectivity. The choice between wired and wireless depends on specific needs, and routers and switches play essential roles in managing data flow within and between networks.

Peripheral Connectivity
1. USB, Thunderbolt, and HDMI:

a. USB (Universal Serial Bus): USB is a widely used standard for connecting various devices to a computer. It supports hot-swapping, allowing devices to be connected or disconnected without restarting the computer.

Types:

USB-A: The standard rectangular USB connector.

USB-B: Square-shaped connectors often found on printers and some older devices.

USB-C: Reversible and versatile connector used in modern devices for data transfer, charging, and video output.

Versatility: USB supports a wide range of devices, including keyboards, mice, external hard drives, printers, and more.

Data Transfer Speeds: USB standards have evolved, with USB 3.0 and later versions providing faster data transfer speeds.

b. Thunderbolt: Thunderbolt is an interface developed by Intel in collaboration with Apple. It combines data transfer, video output, and power delivery through a single cable.

Speed: Thunderbolt offers high data transfer speeds, making it suitable for connecting external storage, displays, and other peripherals.

Daisy Chaining: Thunderbolt allows daisy-chaining multiple devices through a single port, simplifying cable management.

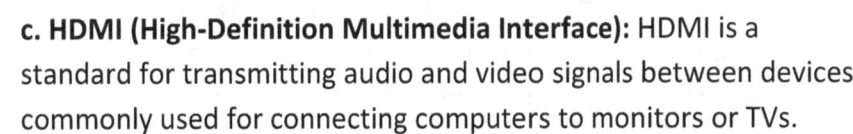

c. HDMI (High-Definition Multimedia Interface): HDMI is a standard for transmitting audio and video signals between devices, commonly used for connecting computers to monitors or TVs.

Audio and Video: HDMI supports both audio and video signals through a single cable.

Resolution Support: HDMI standards have evolved to support higher resolutions, including 4K and beyond.

CEC (Consumer Electronics Control): HDMI often includes CEC, enabling devices to be controlled with a single remote.

2. Device Drivers and Installation: Device drivers are software components that enable the operating system to communicate with and control hardware devices.

Installation Process:

Automatic Installation: Many devices plug-and-play, with the operating system automatically installing necessary drivers upon connection.

Manual Installation: Some devices require manual driver installation. This involves downloading the appropriate driver from the manufacturer's website and installing it on the computer.

Device Manager (Windows):

Access: Device Manager is a Windows tool that allows users to view and manage installed hardware devices.

Driver Updates: Users can update, uninstall, or roll back drivers through Device Manager.

Additional Considerations:

Compatibility: Ensure that drivers are compatible with the operating system version.

Manufacturer Support: Manufacturers regularly release driver updates for improved compatibility and performance.

Conclusion:

Understanding peripheral connectivity options like USB, Thunderbolt, and HDMI provides users with the flexibility to connect a variety of devices to their computers. Additionally, awareness of device drivers and the installation process is essential for ensuring proper communication between the operating system and hardware devices. Whether for data transfer, display connections, or multimedia playback, the right peripheral connectivity choices enhance the overall user experience.

Power Supplies and Cases
Understanding Power Supplies

1. Wattage and Efficiency: Power supplies (PSUs) are essential components in a computer, converting electrical power from an outlet into usable power for the system. Understanding wattage and efficiency is crucial for selecting an appropriate and efficient power supply.

a. Wattage: Wattage represents the amount of power a PSU can deliver to the components in a computer system. It is measured in watts (W).

Selection Considerations:

Components: The total wattage required depends on the power needs of components like the CPU, GPU, drives, and other peripherals.

Overhead: It's advisable to choose a power supply with a wattage slightly higher than the calculated requirement to accommodate future upgrades and ensure system stability.

b. Efficiency: Efficiency refers to how well a power supply converts electrical input from the outlet into usable power for the system. It is expressed as a percentage.

Efficiency Ratings:

80 PLUS Certification: Power supplies are often rated with the 80 PLUS certification, indicating their efficiency. Ratings include 80 PLUS, 80 PLUS Bronze, Silver, Gold, Platinum, and Titanium, with higher ratings signifying greater efficiency.

Benefits of High Efficiency:

Energy Savings: More efficient power supplies waste less energy, resulting in lower electricity bills.

Cooler Operation: Efficient power supplies generate less heat, contributing to cooler overall system temperatures.

2. Modular vs. Non-modular PSUs:

a. Modular Power Supplies: Modular power supplies allow users to detach and attach cables based on their system's requirements. Unused cables can be removed, promoting cleaner cable management.

Benefits:

Cable Management: Modular PSUs help maintain a neat and organized interior by reducing cable clutter.

Improved Airflow: With only necessary cables connected, airflow within the case can be optimized, contributing to better cooling.

Considerations:

Cost: Modular power supplies tend to be slightly more expensive than their non-modular counterparts.

Connectors: Modular PSUs come with connectors for cables, and users must ensure compatibility with their components.

 **b. Non-modular Power Supplies:** Non-modular power supplies have fixed cables that are permanently attached to the unit.

Benefits:

Affordability: Non-modular PSUs are generally more budget-friendly than modular options.

Simplicity: With fixed cables, there is no need to worry about cable compatibility or misplacement.

Considerations:

Cable Management: Cable management may be more challenging due to the fixed cables, leading to a potentially messier interior.

Airflow Considerations: Users need to plan cable routing carefully to avoid obstructing airflow.

Conclusion:

Understanding power supply wattage and efficiency helps users select a PSU that meets the power requirements of their components while ensuring energy efficiency. The choice between modular and non-modular power supplies depends on preferences, budget constraints, and the desire for improved cable management and airflow. A well-chosen power supply contributes to system stability, longevity, and overall performance.

Computer Cases

1. Types and Form Factors: Computer cases house and protect the internal components of a computer. Understanding different types and form factors helps users choose a case that suits their needs and accommodates their hardware.

a. Types of Computer Cases:

Tower Case: Tower cases are vertical, upright cases that come in various sizes, including mid-tower and full-tower.
Characteristics: They provide ample space for components, allowing for efficient cooling and easy accessibility.

Desktop Case: Desktop cases are horizontal and often designed to sit on a desk. They are compact and suitable for small form factor builds.
Characteristics: While they may have limited space for components, they are ideal for space-conscious users.

Cube Case: Cube cases have a cube-shaped design, providing a balance between size and component compatibility.
Characteristics: Cube cases often allow for unique layouts, supporting efficient cooling options.

Mini-ITX Case: Mini-ITX cases are designed for the Mini-ITX motherboard form factor, emphasizing a compact build.
Characteristics: These cases are suitable for small, portable, or HTPC (Home Theater PC) setups.

b. Form Factors:

ATX (Advanced Technology eXtended): ATX is a common motherboard form factor, and cases designed for ATX motherboards are prevalent.
Characteristics: ATX cases offer ample space for components, suitable for standard desktop builds.

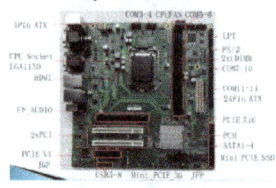

Micro-ATX (mATX): Micro-ATX is a smaller motherboard form factor, and cases designed for mATX motherboards are more compact.

Characteristics: mATX cases are suitable for users who want a smaller footprint without sacrificing too much component space.

Mini-ITX: Mini-ITX is the smallest standard motherboard form factor, and cases for Mini-ITX builds are compact.

Characteristics: Mini-ITX cases are often chosen for small, space-efficient builds with limited internal space.

2. Cable Management: Cable management involves organizing and routing cables within the case to improve airflow, aesthetics, and ease of component maintenance.

Importance of Cable Management:

Airflow: Well-managed cables facilitate better airflow within the case, contributing to improved cooling performance.

Aesthetics: Neat and organized cables enhance the overall look of the build, showcasing components without cable clutter.

Maintenance: Proper cable management makes it easier to access and replace components, reducing the hassle during upgrades or troubleshooting.

Cable Management Techniques:

Cable Routing Channels: Many cases come with built-in channels or routing spaces behind the motherboard tray to guide and hide cables.

Cable Ties and Velcro Straps: Securing cables with ties or straps helps bundle and organize them neatly.

Modular Power Supplies: Modular PSUs allow users to connect only the necessary cables, reducing excess clutter.

Cable Combs: These accessories help align and organize individual cables, especially for power supply and GPU cables.

Tips for Effective Cable Management:

Plan Ahead: Consider cable routing before installing components to optimize placement.

Use Cable Ties or Velcro: Secure cables at various points to keep them organized and prevent tangling.

Group Cables: Bundle similar cables together to create a cleaner and more organized appearance.

Use Cable Combs: For power supply cables, cable combs help maintain a uniform and organized look.

Conclusion:

Understanding the types and form factors of computer cases allows users to choose a case that suits their build preferences and space constraints. Efficient cable management enhances system performance, aesthetics, and maintenance, contributing to an overall well-organized and functional computer setup.

Cooling Systems

1. Case Fans and Airflow: Proper cooling is essential to maintain optimal temperatures within a computer, preventing components from overheating. Case fans and airflow management play a crucial role in dissipating heat efficiently.

a. Case Fans: Case fans circulate air within the computer case, removing hot air and introducing cooler air to keep components at a safe temperature.

Types of Case Fans:

Intake Fans: These fans bring cool air into the case.

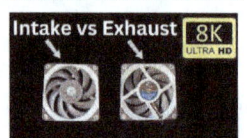

Exhaust Fans: These fans expel hot air from the case.

Top Fans: Positioned on the top of the case, they contribute to heat dissipation.

Side Fans: Mounted on the side panel, side fans can provide additional cooling for specific components.

Airflow Direction:

Positive Airflow: More intake fans than exhaust fans create positive pressure, reducing dust buildup and promoting efficient cooling.

Negative Airflow: More exhaust fans than intake fans create negative pressure, expelling hot air quickly but potentially drawing in more dust.

b. Airflow Management: Proper airflow management ensures that cool air reaches components and hot air is efficiently expelled, preventing heat buildup.

Tips for Airflow Management:

Clear Pathways: Ensure unobstructed pathways for airflow, avoiding cables or components blocking fans.

Strategic Placement: Place intake fans where cool air is needed most, and exhaust fans where hot air accumulates.

Cable Management: Neat cable management helps maintain clear airflow paths and prevents cables from obstructing fans.

Positive and Negative Pressure:

Positive Pressure: Reduces dust buildup but requires careful management to avoid heat pockets.

Negative Pressure: Expels hot air efficiently but may draw in more dust.

2. Liquid Cooling Solutions: Liquid cooling solutions use a closed-loop system to transfer heat away from components more efficiently than air cooling.

a. AIO Liquid Coolers (All-in-One): AIO liquid coolers consist of a pre-filled closed-loop system with a pump, radiator, and water block.

Installation: AIO coolers are easy to install and typically come with universal mounting solutions for various CPU sockets.

Performance: AIO coolers offer effective cooling performance and can be a space-efficient solution.

b. Custom Liquid Cooling: Custom liquid cooling setups involve individually selecting components like pumps, reservoirs, radiators, tubing, and water blocks.

Installation: Custom setups require more effort and expertise in building and maintenance.

Performance: Custom liquid cooling can provide superior cooling performance, especially in high-performance and overclocked systems.

Advantages of Liquid Cooling:

Efficiency: Liquid cooling can transfer heat more efficiently than air cooling, leading to lower component temperatures.

Aesthetics: Liquid cooling setups can be visually appealing, especially in custom builds with colored coolant and RGB lighting.

Noise Level: Liquid cooling systems can be quieter than some high-performance air coolers.

Considerations:

Cost: AIO coolers are generally more affordable than custom liquid cooling setups.
Maintenance: Custom liquid cooling requires periodic maintenance, including checking for leaks and topping up coolant.

Conclusion:

Understanding case fans, airflow management, and liquid cooling solutions is crucial for maintaining a computer's optimal temperature and performance. Whether using air cooling with strategically placed case fans or opting for liquid cooling for enhanced efficiency, proper cooling contributes to the longevity and stability of computer components. Users should choose a cooling solution based on their specific needs, system requirements, and level of expertise.

<u>Troubleshooting and Maintenance</u>
Basic Troubleshooting Techniques
1. Common Issues and Solutions:

a. Computer Not Turning On:

Possible Causes:

Power supply issues.

Loose cables or connections.

Faulty motherboard or components.

Solutions: Check power cables and connections.

Test the power outlet.

Ensure the power supply switch is on.

If possible, test with a different power supply.

b. Slow Performance:

Possible Causes: Insufficient RAM.

Too many background processes.

Malware or viruses.

Solutions: Check and upgrade RAM if needed.

Close unnecessary background applications.

Run antivirus and anti-malware scans.

c. No Display on Monitor:

Possible Causes: Loose monitor cables.

Graphics card issues.

Monitor or graphics driver problems.

Solutions: Check and secure monitor cables.

Test with a different monitor.

Update or reinstall graphics drivers.

d. Internet Connection Issues:

Possible Causes:

Router or modem problems.

Network cable issues.

ISP (Internet Service Provider) problems.

Solutions: Restart router and modem.

Check network cables.

Contact ISP for assistance.

e. Blue Screen of Death (BSOD):

Possible Causes:

Hardware or driver issues.

Memory problems.

Operating system errors.

Solutions: Update or reinstall problematic drivers.

Check for memory issues using diagnostic tools.

Perform a system restore or reinstall the operating system.

2. Diagnostic Tools and Software:

a. Windows Troubleshooter: Windows has built-in troubleshooters for various issues, including network problems, hardware, and Windows Update.

Usage: Access Troubleshooters in Windows settings.

Run the relevant troubleshooter for the specific issue.

b. Task Manager: Task Manager provides real-time information about running processes, CPU usage, memory usage, and more.

Usage: Press Ctrl + Shift + Esc to open Task Manager.

Identify and close resource-intensive processes.

c. Event Viewer: Event Viewer logs events and errors on your system, helping identify the cause of issues.

Usage: Search for "Event Viewer" in the Start menu.

Examine logs for errors or warnings.

d. Disk Cleanup: Disk Cleanup helps free up disk space by removing temporary files, system files, and other unnecessary data.

Usage: Search for "Disk Cleanup" in the Start menu.

Select the drive to clean and follow the prompts.

e. System File Checker (SFC): SFC scans and repairs corrupted system files that may cause issues.

Usage: Open Command Prompt as administrator.

Type sfc /scannow and press Enter.

f. Antivirus and Anti-Malware Scans: Use reputable antivirus and anti-malware software to scan for and remove malicious threats.

Usage: Run scheduled or manual scans with the installed security software.

Conclusion:

Basic troubleshooting involves identifying and addressing common computer issues using simple solutions. Diagnostic tools and software, along with a systematic approach to problem-solving, can help users resolve issues efficiently. Regular maintenance and staying informed about common problems contribute to a smoother and more reliable computing experience.

Software and Firmware Updates

1. Importance and Process:

a. Importance of Updates: Updates often include patches for vulnerabilities, enhancing the system's security and protecting it from potential threats.

Performance: Updates may optimize software or firmware, improving performance, fixing bugs, and introducing new features.

Compatibility: Keeping software and firmware up to date ensures compatibility with the latest hardware and technologies.

Reliability: Updates can address stability issues, reducing the likelihood of crashes or system failures.

b. Update Process:

Automatic Updates: Many software applications and operating systems offer automatic updates, ensuring that users receive the latest patches and features without manual intervention.

Manual Updates: Some software and firmware updates require manual initiation. Users should periodically check for updates and follow the provided instructions.

Best Practices: Create backups before major updates to safeguard important data. Check release notes or update descriptions for information on changes and improvements.

Ensure a stable internet connection during the update process.

2. BIOS and Driver Updates:

a. BIOS Updates: The BIOS (Basic Input/Output System) is firmware that initializes hardware components during the system boot process.

Importance:

Compatibility: BIOS updates often address compatibility issues with new hardware.

Security: Some updates include security enhancements.

Performance: BIOS updates may improve system stability and performance.

Update Process: Identify Current BIOS Version: Check the current BIOS version in the system.

Download the Update: Visit the motherboard manufacturer's website to download the latest BIOS update.

Flash the BIOS: Follow the manufacturer's instructions to flash the BIOS using a USB drive or specialized software.

b. Driver Updates: Drivers are software components that enable communication between the operating system and hardware devices.

Importance:

Performance: Updated drivers can enhance hardware performance.

Bug Fixes: Driver updates often address known issues and bugs.

Compatibility: New drivers may improve compatibility with the latest software and hardware.

Update Process:

Identify Drivers: Identify the hardware components for which updated drivers are available.

Download Drivers: Visit the manufacturer's website or use automatic driver update tools to download the latest drivers.

Installation: Follow the installation instructions provided by the manufacturer.

Automatic Driver Updates: Some operating systems and driver management tools offer automatic driver updates.

Users can enable automatic updates to ensure that drivers are kept up to date.

Conclusion:

Regularly updating software and firmware is crucial for maintaining system security, stability, and performance. Users should stay informed about available updates, check release notes for details, and follow best practices to ensure a smooth update process. Updating BIOS and drivers contributes to a more reliable and efficient computing experience.

Preventative Maintenance

1. Cleaning and Dust Removal:

a. Importance of Cleaning:

Efficient Cooling: Dust buildup inside a computer can obstruct airflow, leading to increased temperatures and potential overheating of components.

System Reliability: Regular cleaning reduces the risk of hardware failures caused by dust accumulation on sensitive components.

Aesthetics: Keeping the computer clean enhances its appearance and makes troubleshooting and maintenance more accessible.

b. Cleaning Process:

Exterior Cleaning: Wipe the exterior surfaces with a soft, lint-free cloth.

Use a gentle cleaner for stubborn stains, avoiding harsh chemicals.

Interior Cleaning: Power off the computer and disconnect all cables.

Use compressed air to blow out dust from components like fans, heatsinks, and power supply.

Be cautious around delicate components, and prevent fans from spinning while cleaning.

Monitor and Peripherals: Clean monitors with appropriate screen cleaning solutions.

Wipe down peripherals such as keyboards and mice regularly to prevent dust and debris buildup.

Frequency: Perform cleaning every 3-6 months, or more frequently if the environment is dusty.

2. Component Lifespan and Upgrades:

a. Understanding Component Lifespan:

Components with Limited Lifespan: Mechanical components like hard drives and fans may have a finite lifespan.

Batteries in laptops and some motherboards also degrade over time.

Factors Affecting Lifespan:

Heat: Excessive heat can shorten the lifespan of components.

Usage: Components used intensively may wear out faster.

b. Upgrades for Extended Lifespan:

Hardware Upgrades:

Storage: Consider upgrading to a solid-state drive (SSD) for improved performance and reliability.

Memory (RAM): Adding more RAM can enhance multitasking capabilities and overall system responsiveness.

Regular Backups: Regularly back up important data to prevent loss in case of hardware failure.

Cooling Solutions: Install additional or more efficient cooling solutions to maintain lower temperatures.

Optimization: Periodically optimize software and remove unnecessary programs to reduce strain on components.

Environmental Considerations: Ensure the computer is placed in a well-ventilated area with minimal dust.

c. Upgrade Considerations:

Compatibility: Ensure that upgrades are compatible with existing components.

Budget: Plan upgrades based on budget constraints and the cost-effectiveness of extending the system's lifespan.

Performance Needs: Evaluate whether upgrades align with the user's performance needs and usage patterns.

Conclusion:

Preventative maintenance, including regular cleaning and addressing component lifespan considerations, is crucial for ensuring the longevity and reliability of a computer system. Taking proactive measures to reduce dust buildup, upgrading components strategically, and practicing good environmental habits contribute to an optimized and long-lasting computing experience.

Advanced Topics and Emerging Trends

Emerging Hardware Technologies

1. Quantum Computing: Quantum computing is a revolutionary approach to computation that leverages the principles of quantum mechanics.

Quantum Bits (Qubits): Classical computers use bits (0s and 1s) for processing information.

Quantum computers use qubits, which can exist in multiple states simultaneously due to superposition.

Entanglement: Qubits can be entangled, meaning the state of one qubit is directly related to the state of another, regardless of the physical distance between them.

Importance and Applications:

Computational Power: Quantum computers have the potential to perform certain types of calculations exponentially faster than classical computers.

Applications: Quantum computing holds promise for solving complex problems in fields such as cryptography, optimization, drug discovery, and materials science.

c. Current State:

Challenges: Quantum computers are still in the early stages of development and face challenges such as maintaining qubit stability and minimizing errors.

Companies and Research: Major companies and research institutions are actively working on developing practical quantum computers, with progress being made in both hardware and algorithms.

2. Neuromorphic Hardware: Neuromorphic hardware is inspired by the structure and functioning of the human brain's neural networks.

Parallel Processing: Neuromorphic hardware focuses on parallel processing, allowing multiple operations to be performed simultaneously, mimicking the brain's efficiency.

Synapses and Neurons: Neuromorphic systems use artificial neurons and synapses to replicate the interconnected nature of biological neural networks.

b. Importance and Applications:

Efficiency in AI and Machine Learning: Neuromorphic hardware is designed to accelerate tasks related to artificial intelligence (AI) and machine learning by efficiently handling complex, interconnected data.

Pattern Recognition: Applications include tasks such as pattern recognition, sensory processing, and other AI functions that benefit from the parallel and distributed processing inherent in biological neural networks.

c. Current State:

Research and Development: Neuromorphic hardware is an active area of research, with both academic institutions and tech companies exploring its potential applications.

Integration with AI: As AI and machine learning continue to advance, there is growing interest in integrating neuromorphic hardware to enhance the efficiency of AI algorithms.

Conclusion:

Quantum computing and neuromorphic hardware represent two groundbreaking technologies with the potential to reshape the landscape of computation. While both are still in the early stages of development, ongoing research and advancements hold the promise of unlocking new capabilities and addressing complex challenges in computing, artificial intelligence, and other fields. As these technologies mature, they are likely to play a significant role in shaping the future of hardware and computational capabilities.

Green Computing

1. Energy-efficient Hardware:

a. Overview:

Definition: Green computing, also known as eco-friendly computing, focuses on reducing the environmental impact of computing technologies.

Energy Consumption: Traditional computing devices can consume significant amounts of energy during operation.

b. Energy-efficient Hardware:

Low-power Components: and producing hardware Manufacturers are designing components with lower power consumption, including processors, graphics cards, and storage devices.

Energy Star Certification: Energy Star is a certification program that identifies energy-efficient products, providing consumers with information to make environmentally conscious choices.

Efficient Cooling Solutions: Improved cooling solutions, such as more efficient fans and heat sinks, contribute to reducing overall energy consumption.

c. Importance and Benefits:

Environmental Impact: Energy-efficient hardware reduces the carbon footprint associated with computing devices, lowering overall greenhouse gas emissions.

Cost Savings: Energy-efficient components can result in lower electricity bills for both individual users and organizations.

Regulatory Compliance: Many regions and countries have regulations or incentives for using energy-efficient technologies, encouraging businesses to adopt green computing practices.

2. E-waste Management:

a. Overview:

Definition: E-waste, or electronic waste, refers to discarded electronic devices and components.

Growing Challenge: The rapid pace of technological advancements contributes to a growing amount of e-waste globally.

b. E-waste Management:

Recycling Programs: Governments, organizations, and manufacturers are implementing e-waste recycling programs to responsibly dispose of electronic devices.

Refurbishment and Reuse: Devices in good condition can be refurbished and reused, extending their lifespan and reducing the need for new manufacturing.

Awareness and Education: Promoting awareness about e-waste and educating consumers about proper disposal methods are crucial aspects of effective e-waste management.

c. Importance and Benefits:

Toxic Materials: Electronic devices often contain hazardous materials, such as lead and mercury. Proper disposal prevents these materials from harming the environment and human health.

Resource Conservation: Recycling e-waste helps recover valuable resources, including metals, reducing the need for raw material extraction and processing.

Circular Economy: Adopting a circular economy approach encourages the reuse and recycling of electronic components, minimizing waste and promoting sustainable practices.

Conclusion:

Green computing emphasizes the importance of reducing the environmental impact of technology. Energy-efficient hardware choices and effective e-waste management are critical components of this approach. By adopting energy-efficient technologies and responsibly managing electronic waste, individuals and organizations can contribute to a more sustainable and environmentally friendly computing ecosystem.

Hands-on Project

1. Build and Configure a Computer System:

a. Planning:

Define Purpose: Determine the primary use of the computer (e.g., gaming, content creation, office tasks) to guide component selection.

Budgeting: Establish a budget for the project, considering the cost of components such as the CPU, GPU, RAM, storage, motherboard, and peripherals.

b. Component Selection:

Processor (CPU): Choose a CPU based on performance requirements and budget.

Graphics Card (GPU): Select a GPU suitable for the intended use (gaming, graphic design, etc.).

Memory (RAM): Choose RAM based on system requirements and multitasking needs.

Storage: Decide on storage options (SSD for speed, HDD for larger storage).

Motherboard: Choose a motherboard compatible with the CPU and other components.

Power Supply (PSU): Select a PSU with sufficient wattage and efficiency for the system.

Case: Choose a case based on form factor, aesthetics, and airflow considerations.

c. Building:

Static Precautions: Work on an anti-static mat or use an anti-static wrist strap to prevent static electricity damage.

CPU and RAM Installation: Install the CPU and RAM on the motherboard.

Mounting Components: Secure the motherboard, install the GPU, connect storage drives, and attach the power supply.

Cable Management: Organize and route cables neatly to improve airflow and aesthetics.

Peripheral Setup: Connect peripherals such as the monitor, keyboard, and mouse.

d. BIOS Configuration:

Accessing BIOS : Boot the system and access the BIOS/UEFI firmware.

Settings Configuration: Configure settings such as boot order, system date and time, and hardware-specific settings.

OS Installation: Install the operating system (OS) using a USB drive or installation disc.

Driver Installation: Install necessary drivers for components, such as graphics and motherboard drivers.

2. Troubleshoot and Optimize Performance:

a. Troubleshooting:

Boot Issues: Check connections, ensure components are seated properly, and troubleshoot any boot-related problems.

Hardware Compatibility: Verify that all components are compatible, especially concerning the motherboard and CPU.

Operating System Errors: Address any OS-related errors through troubleshooting and, if necessary, reinstall the OS.

b. Performance Optimization:

BIOS/UEFI Updates: Check the motherboard manufacturer's website for BIOS/UEFI updates to improve system stability and compatibility.

Driver Updates: Update graphics, chipset, and other drivers to ensure optimal performance.

Overclocking (Optional): If desired, explore overclocking the CPU or GPU for enhanced performance. Be cautious and monitor temperatures.

Monitoring Tools: Use monitoring tools to track temperatures, fan speeds, and system resource usage.

Benchmarking: Run benchmarks to assess system performance and identify potential bottlenecks.

c. Temperature Management:

Airflow Assessment: Evaluate the case's airflow and adjust fan configurations if necessary.

Cooling Solutions: Consider additional cooling solutions, such as aftermarket CPU coolers or case fans, for temperature optimization.

Dust Management: Regularly clean dust from components to prevent overheating.

d. System Maintenance:

Backup Solutions: Implement a regular backup strategy to safeguard important data.

Security Software: Install and update antivirus and anti-malware software for system security.

Regular Updates: Keep the OS, drivers, and software up to date to benefit from performance improvements and security patches.

Conclusion:

Building and configuring a computer system involves careful planning, component selection, and hands-on assembly. Troubleshooting and optimizing performance require attention to detail and ongoing maintenance. This hands-on project provides valuable experience in creating a functional, optimized, and well-maintained computer system.

Assessment and Evaluation:

Weekly Quizzes and Assignments

Computer Hardware Basics:

1. What does computer hardware refer to?

a. Software components

b. Tangible components

c. Virtual components

d. Internet components

2. What is the main function of the Central Processing Unit (CPU)?

a. Stores files

b. Processes data

c. Manages power supply

d. Connects components

3. Where does the computer keep data it's currently using?

a. Hard Disk Drive (HDD)

b. Solid State Drive (SSD)

c. RAM (Memory)

d. CPU Cache

4. What is the purpose of storage in a computer?

a. Provides power

b. Executes instructions

c. Stores files and software

d. Allows quick data access

5. What is the function of the motherboard?

a. Provides pathways for data and power distribution

b. Processes data

c. Converts electrical current

d. Stores temporary data

6. What component provides electrical power to the computer?

a. CPU

b. RAM

c. Power Supply Unit (PSU)

d. Motherboard

History and Evolution of Computers:

7. What is one of the earliest known calculating tools?

a. Mechanical Calculator

b. Abacus

c. Analytical Engine

d. ENIAC

8. In which era did transistors revolutionize electronics and computing?

a. 1600s-1800s

b. 1950s

c. 1970s

d. 1990s-2000s

9. Which device is considered the "brain" of the computer?

a. Motherboard

b. CPU

c. RAM

d. SSD

10. What did the IBM PC (1981) set standards for in the computing industry?

a. Gaming

b. Software compatibility

c. Cloud computing

d. Mobile devices

11. What did the Apple I (1976) play a pivotal role in developing?

a. Smartphones

b. Home computing

c. Mainframe computers

d. Artificial intelligence

12. What is the main significance of Cloud Computing in the 2010s?

a. Making computers smaller

b. Revolutionizing work and communication

c. Pioneering electronic computing

d. Developing powerful supercomputers

General Understanding:

13. Why is understanding computer hardware important?

a. For cooking

b. For gardening

c. For using a computer effectively

d. For playing sports

14. Who is likely to benefit from knowing computer hardware basics?

a. Only IT professionals

b. Only children

c. Anyone using a computer

d. Only gamers

15. What analogy is used to explain how computer components work together?

a. Ocean waves

b. Busy office

c. Mountain climbing

d. Space exploration

16. What role does the CPU play in the analogy of a busy office?

a. Manager

b. Desk space

c. Filing cabinets

d. Office floor plan

17. Why would someone need to upgrade their computer hardware?

a. To make coffee

b. To troubleshoot problems

c. To watch TV

d. To learn a new language

18. Which component provides electrical power to the computer?

a. Monitor

b. Power Supply Unit (PSU)

c. Mouse

d. Keyboard

19. What is the primary function of storage in a computer?

a. Providing power

b. Executing instructions

c. Storing files and software

d. Allowing quick data access

20. In the history of computers, which device is considered one of the earliest tools for mathematical calculations?

a. Mechanical Calculator

b. Analytical Engine

c. ENIAC

d. Abacus

Assignment 1:
Hardware Components Identification

Task: Identify and label the major hardware components of a computer system.

Components to identify: CPU, RAM, HDD/SSD, Motherboard, PSU, Input devices (keyboard, mouse), Output devices (monitor, printer).

Submission: Submit a labeled diagram or a written list highlighting the identified components.

Assignment 2:
Computer Hardware Comparison

Task: Compare the features and functions of a traditional HDD and an SSD.

Aspects to consider: Speed, durability, storage capacity, and cost.

Submission: Write a short essay or create a comparison chart highlighting the differences between HDDs and SSDs.

Assignment 3:
The Role of the Motherboard

Task: Explain the role of the motherboard in a computer system.

Topics to cover: Data and power distribution, connectivity, and how the motherboard connects various components.

Submission: Write a short essay or create a presentation explaining the functions of a motherboard.

Assignment 4:
Power Supply and Electricity Basics

Task: Research and explain how the Power Supply Unit (PSU) works and the basics of electrical currents.

Topics to cover: Voltage, current, power, and how the PSU converts electrical current for computer components.

Submission: Create a simple infographic or a written explanation on PSU and electrical basics.

Assignment 5:
Importance of Understanding Computer Hardware

Task: Reflect on the importance of understanding computer hardware for everyday users and IT professionals.

Topics to cover: Informed decision-making for upgrades, troubleshooting, and optimizing performance.

Submission: Write a short essay expressing your thoughts on the significance of computer hardware knowledge.

These assignments aim to reinforce the understanding of computer hardware concepts in a simple and practical way.

Supercomputers:

1. What are supercomputers designed for?
2. What is a key feature of supercomputers related to processing speed?

Mainframe Computers:

3. Where are mainframe computers commonly used?
4. What distinguishes mainframe computers in terms of user support?

Minicomputers (Midrange Computers):

5. What is another name for minicomputers?
6. What type of business operations are minicomputers suitable for?

Microcomputers (Personal Computers):

7. What is the common name for microcomputers?

8. What is the primary purpose of personal computers?

Workstations:

9. What applications are workstations optimized for?
10. How do workstations differ from standard personal computers?

Embedded Computers:

11. Where are embedded computers integrated?
12. What type of devices often use embedded computers?

General Classification:

13. How does computer classification help in decision-making?
14. What aspects can computers be classified based on?

Supercomputers vs. Personal Computers:

15. What distinguishes supercomputers from personal computers in terms of processing capabilities?
16. In which scenarios are personal computers more commonly used?

Mainframe vs. Minicomputers:

17. What characterizes the usage of mainframe computers compared to minicomputers?
18. How does user support differ between mainframes and minicomputers?

Microcomputers vs. Workstations:

19. How do microcomputers differ from workstations in terms of performance?
20. For what types of tasks are workstations better suited than microcomputers?

Supercomputers:

Assignment 1:

Research and list three real-world applications where supercomputers are used, explaining their significance.

Assignment 2:

Compare the processing speed of a supercomputer with that of a typical personal computer. What makes supercomputers faster?

Mainframe Computers:

Assignment 3:

Investigate the role of mainframe computers in the banking industry. How are they utilized for transaction processing?

Assignment 4:

Discuss the importance of extensive memory and storage capacities in mainframe computers for large enterprises.

Minicomputers (Midrange Computers):

Assignment 5:

Identify two industries where minicomputers are commonly employed. Explain how their moderate processing capabilities are beneficial.

Assignment 6:

Explore the concept of scalable architecture in minicomputers and its impact on adapting to changing business needs.

Microcomputers (Personal Computers):

Assignment 7:

Create a comparison chart highlighting the differences between desktops, laptops, and tablets as types of microcomputers.

Assignment 8:

Investigate the evolution of personal computers and how they have become integral to daily life.

Workstations:

Assignment 9:

Explore the use of workstations in the field of graphic design or scientific research. What features make them suitable for these tasks?

Assignment 10:

Discuss the significance of specialized hardware configurations in workstations for professionals.

Embedded Computers:

Assignment 11:

Investigate how embedded computers contribute to the functionality of IoT devices in smart homes.

Assignment 12:

Discuss the challenges and benefits of designing compact and energy-efficient embedded systems for specific applications.

Servers Quizzes and Assignments

Web Servers:

1. What does HTTP stand for, and what is its role in web servers?

2. Name one security feature commonly used in web servers to encrypt data during communication.

File Servers:

3. Explain the main purpose of a file server in a network.

4. Mention one file sharing protocol used by file servers, and describe its function.

Database Servers:

5. What is the role of a database server in managing data?

6. Name a feature of database servers that ensures the security and integrity of stored data.

Application Servers:

7. Describe the primary function of an application server.

8. What are middleware services, and why are they essential for application servers?

Mail Servers:

9. What is the responsibility of a mail server in handling email communication?

10. Name two email protocols and briefly explain their purposes.

Virtual Servers (Virtual Machines):

11. Define virtualization technology and its role in virtual servers.

12. How does virtualization provide flexibility in server deployment and scaling?

General Server Knowledge:

13. What is the primary purpose of servers in a network environment?

14. How do servers facilitate collaboration among computers and devices?

Security Aspects:

15. Why is SSL/TLS encryption important for web servers?

16. Mention one security measure employed by mail servers to control user access.

Resource Management:

17. How does resource allocation work in virtual servers?

18. Explain the significance of user access control in file servers.

Protocols and Standards:

19. Name a protocol used for email routing, and outline its function.

20. Which protocol is commonly associated with file sharing in Windows environments?

Server Systems Assignments

Web Servers:

Assignment 1:

Research and list three security measures, other than SSL/TLS encryption, that web servers can implement to protect websites.

File Servers:

Assignment 2:

Explain the importance of data backup and recovery in file servers. Provide a scenario illustrating when this feature could be crucial.

Database Servers:

Assignment 3:

Compare and contrast two popular database management systems (DBMS) used by database servers, highlighting their key features and use cases.

Application Servers:

Assignment 4:

Create a presentation on the role of application servers in supporting the deployment and execution of business applications. Include examples of applications commonly hosted on such servers.

Mail Servers:
Assignment 5:

Investigate and summarize the differences between the SMTP, IMAP, and POP3 email protocols. Discuss their specific roles in mail servers.

Virtual Servers (Virtual Machines):
Assignment 6:

Write a report on the benefits of virtualization technology in terms of resource efficiency, cost savings, and environmental impact. Include real-world examples where virtual servers excel.

General Server Knowledge:
Assignment 7:

Interview an IT professional or conduct online research to explore the evolving role of servers in modern computing environments. Present your findings in a short essay.

Security Aspects:
Assignment 8:

Develop a security checklist for server administrators, outlining essential practices to safeguard server environments. Include measures for both physical and digital security.

Resource Management:
Assignment 9:

Create a flowchart or diagram illustrating the process of resource allocation and management in virtual servers. Explain each step.

Protocols and Standards:
Assignment 10:

Explore emerging server communication protocols or standards. Write a brief analysis of their potential impact on improving server performance and security.

Understanding Motherboards Quiz and Assignment

CPU Socket Quiz:

1. Where is the CPU typically installed on the motherboard?

A. RAM Slots

B. Expansion Slots

C. CPU Socket

D. Storage Interfaces

RAM Slots Quiz:

2. What is the main function of RAM slots on a motherboard?

A. CPU Installation

B. Permanent Data Storage

C. Temporary Data Storage

D. Graphics Card Connection

Expansion Slots Quiz:

3. Which type of slot allows you to add a graphics card to enhance your computer's performance?

A. USB Slot

B. RAM Slot

C. Expansion Slot

D. Networking Port

Storage Interfaces Quiz:

4. What do SATA and M.2 connectors on a motherboard enable you to connect?

A. Graphics Cards

B. Storage Devices

C. Network Adapters

D. External Monitors

Connectors and Ports Quiz:

5. Which of the following is NOT a connector or port found on a motherboard?

A. USB

B. HDMI

C. Graphics Card Slot

D. Networking Port

ATX Form Factor Quiz:

6. What does ATX stand for in the context of motherboard form factors?

A. Advanced Technology eXtended

B. All Types eXpanded

C. Advanced Tool eXperience

D. Accessory Terminal eXchange

Micro-ATX and Mini-ITX Quiz:

7. Which form factor is suitable for compact and space-constrained systems?

A. ATX

B. Micro-ATX

C. Mini-ITX

D. EATX

Server and Workstation Form Factors Quiz:

8. What form factor is often used for high-performance computing and server systems?

A. ATX

B. Mini-ITX

C. EATX

D. Micro-ATX

BIOS/UEFI Quiz:

9. What does BIOS stand for in the context of motherboard firmware?

A. Basic Input/Output System

B. Backup Internet Operating System

C. Binary Input/Output Setup

D. Base Input/Output Software

Firmware Updates Quiz:

10. Why are firmware updates for BIOS/UEFI important?

A. To enhance compatibility, performance, security, and functionality.

B. To update the operating system.

C. To change the motherboard form factor.

D. To connect external devices.

Motherboard Components Quiz:

11. Which component connects additional cards like sound or network adapters to the motherboard?

A. CPU Socket

B. Expansion Slots

C. RAM Slots

D. Storage Interfaces

UEFI vs. BIOS Quiz:

12. What is the modern replacement for traditional BIOS?

A. UEFI

B. RAID

C. SATA

D. USB

Peripheral Connections Quiz:

13. What are USB, HDMI, and audio jacks examples of on a motherboard?

A. CPU Sockets

B. Storage Interfaces

C. Connectors and Ports

D. Expansion Slots

Motherboard Sizes Quiz:

14. Which form factor is designed for space-constrained systems?

A. ATX

B. Mini-ITX

C. EATX

D. Micro-ATX

Server Motherboards Quiz:

15. What form factor is commonly used for server and workstation motherboards?

A. Micro-ATX

B. EATX

C. Mini-ITX

D. ATX

CPU Installation Quiz:

16. Where is the CPU installed on the motherboard?

A. Expansion Slots

B. RAM Slots

C. CPU Socket

D. Storage Interfaces

Data Storage Quiz:

17. What is the primary purpose of storage interfaces like SATA on a motherboard?

A. Graphics Processing

B. Temporary Data Storage

C. Data Retrieval

D. Permanent Data Storage

Peripheral Connectivity Quiz:

18. What role do connectors and ports play on a motherboard?

A. Graphics Card Connection

B. Temporary Data Storage

C. Connecting External Devices

D. CPU Installation

RAM Functionality Quiz:

19. What is the main function of RAM slots on a motherboard?

A. Storing Operating System Files

B. Temporary Data Storage

C. Permanent Data Storage

D. Graphics Processing

Form Factor Definitions Quiz:

20. In motherboard terminology, what does "Form Factor" refer to?

A. Size, layout, and mounting points.

B. CPU Processing Speed.

C. The number of RAM slots.

D. Networking Capabilities.

Assignment:
Understanding Motherboards
Section 1:
Multiple Choice Questions
CPU Socket:

1. Where is the CPU typically installed on the motherboard?

A. RAM Slots

B. Expansion Slots

C. CPU Socket

D. Storage Interfaces

RAM Slots:

2. What is the primary function of RAM slots on a motherboard?

A. CPU Installation

B. Permanent Data Storage

C. Temporary Data Storage

D. Graphics Card Connection

Expansion Slots:

3. Which slots allow the installation of additional cards like graphics and sound cards?

A. USB Slots

B. RAM Slots

C. Expansion Slots

D. Networking Ports

Storage Interfaces:

4. What do SATA and M.2 connectors enable on a motherboard?

A. Graphics Processing

B. Temporary Data Storage

C. Networking

D. Storage Device Connection

Connectors and Ports:

5. What role do connectors and ports play on a motherboard?

A. Temporary Data Storage

B. Graphics Card Connection

C. Connecting External Devices

D. CPU Installation

Section 2:

True/False Statements
ATX Form Factor:

1. ATX stands for Advanced Technology eXtended.
2. ATX is a form factor commonly used in server systems.

Micro-ATX and Mini-ITX:

3. Micro-ATX and Mini-ITX are larger form factors suitable for gaming PCs.
4. These form factors are designed for space-constrained systems.

Server and Workstation Form Factors:

5. EATX is a form factor commonly used in server and workstation motherboards.
6. Server form factors prioritize compact designs over performance.

Section 3:
Definitions
BIOS/UEFI:

1. Define BIOS.
2. What does UEFI stand for, and how does it differ from BIOS?

Firmware Updates:

3. Explain why motherboard manufacturers release firmware updates.
4. What precautions should be taken during the installation of firmware updates?

Section 4:
Short Answers
Role of Expansion Slots:

Explain the role of expansion slots on a motherboard and provide an example of a card that can be installed in these slots.

Form Factor Selection:

When building a compact PC for a home theater setup, which form factor (Micro-ATX or Mini-ITX) would you choose, and why?

Server Motherboards:

What specific features might you find on a server motherboard that differentiate it from a standard desktop motherboard?

BIOS vs. UEFI:

Briefly compare the traditional BIOS with the modern UEFI in terms of functionality and advantages.

Connectivity Options:

Name three types of connectors or ports found on motherboards and describe their respective functions.

Section 5:
Practical Application
Motherboard Selection:

Imagine you are building a gaming PC. What factors would you consider when selecting a motherboard, and what specific features would you prioritize?

System Stability:

How can regularly updating firmware contribute to the stability and security of a computer system?

Expansion Card Installation:

Outline the general steps involved in installing an expansion card, such as a graphics card, on a motherboard.

Compact System Design:

Discuss the challenges and advantages of designing a compact PC using the Mini-ITX form factor.

Troubleshooting:

List three common issues related to motherboard components and suggest potential troubleshooting steps for each.

Chipset and Slots Quiz and Assignments

Quiz on Chipset and Expansion Slots
Section 1:
Multiple Choice Questions
Chipset Functionality:

1. What is the primary role of the chipset on a motherboard?

A. Connect peripherals to the CPU

B. Manage data flow between components

C. Control the power supply

D. Provide external storage interfaces

Northbridge and Southbridge:

2. Which component of the chipset traditionally connects the CPU to high-speed components like RAM?

A. Northbridge

B. Southbridge

C. PCIe

D. AGP

Expansion Slots:

3. What is the purpose of expansion slots on a motherboard?

A. Increase CPU speed

B. Connect external power sources

C. Accommodate expansion cards

D. Manage cooling systems

PCIe Slot:

4. What type of devices is commonly connected to a PCIe slot?

A. USB Controllers

B. Graphics Cards

C. Sound Cards

D. Storage Devices

Section 2:

True/False Statements

Northbridge and Southbridge:

1. The Northbridge manages high-speed peripherals like RAM.

2. The Southbridge is responsible for high-performance components like graphics cards.

PCIe Slot:

3. PCIe offers higher bandwidth compared to PCI.

4. PCIe slots are primarily used for connecting storage devices.

AGP Slot:

5. AGP is a modern expansion slot commonly found in current motherboards.

6. AGP is specifically designed for connecting networking adapters.

Section 3: Definitions

Northbridge:

1. Explain the role of the Northbridge in the chipset.

PCIe:

2. Define PCIe and mention one advantage it has over PCI.

Expansion Slots:

3. What is the main purpose of expansion slots, and how do they contribute to system customization?

Section 4:

Short Answers

Chipset Components:

List two types of components typically managed by the Southbridge.

AGP Slot Relevance:

Briefly explain why AGP slots are less relevant in modern computer systems.

Upgrade Possibilities:

How do expansion slots enhance a user's ability to upgrade and customize their computer?

Section 5:

Practical Application

Motherboard Selection:

When building a gaming PC, which type of expansion slots would you prioritize, and why?

Compatibility Issues:

Can using an outdated expansion card with a modern motherboard cause compatibility issues? Explain.

Chipset Impact on Performance:

Discuss how a well-designed chipset can positively impact overall system performance.

Expansion Slot Utilization:

Provide examples of two different types of expansion cards and their respective uses in a computer system.

Future-Proofing Considerations:

When buying a motherboard, why might considering the type and number of expansion slots be important for future upgrades?

Assignment:
Understanding Chipset and Expansion Slots
Section 1: Define and Explain
Define Chipset:

In your own words, define what a chipset is and its role in a computer system.
Chipset Functionality:
Explain the primary functionality of a chipset, highlighting its role in managing data flow and coordinating interactions within a computer system.

Northbridge and Southbridge:

Define Northbridge and Southbridge, specifying the responsibilities of each in the context of a motherboard's chipset.

Expansion Slots:

Describe the purpose of expansion slots on a motherboard and how they contribute to the customization and upgrading of a computer system.

PCIe Advantages:

Explain why PCIe (PCI Express) is commonly used for high-performance peripherals, outlining its advantages over traditional PCI slots.

Section 2:
Classify and Compare
Chipset Types:

Compare and contrast Northbridge and Southbridge, highlighting the types of components and peripherals each is responsible for managing.

Expansion Slot Types:

Classify PCI, PCIe, and AGP based on their characteristics, use cases, and relevance in modern computer systems.

Section 3:
Practical Application
Upgrading Systems:

Provide a scenario where a user might utilize expansion slots to upgrade their computer system. Mention the type of expansion card(s) they might use and the benefits of this upgrade.

Compatibility Considerations:

Discuss why understanding the compatibility between a motherboard's chipset and expansion cards is crucial before making upgrades. Provide an example scenario.

Section 4:
Critical Thinking
Future of Expansion Slots:

Share your perspective on the future of expansion slots. Do you think they will remain relevant in upcoming computer architectures? Justify your opinion.

Impact of Chipset Design:

Discuss how a well-designed chipset can impact not only system performance but also the overall user experience. Provide examples or real-world implications.

Section 5:
Reflection
Personal Experience:

Reflect on a personal experience where understanding chipset architecture and expansion slots played a crucial role in a computer-related decision or issue resolution.

Basic Input/Output Systems (BIOS) Quiz and Assignments

Assignment:
Understanding Chipset and Expansion Slots
Section 1: Define and Explain
Define Chipset:

In your own words, define what a chipset is and its role in a computer system.

Chipset Functionality:

Explain the primary functionality of a chipset, highlighting its role in managing data flow and coordinating interactions within a computer system.

Northbridge and Southbridge:

Define Northbridge and Southbridge, specifying the responsibilities of each in the context of a motherboard's chipset.

Expansion Slots:

Describe the purpose of expansion slots on a motherboard and how they contribute to the customization and upgrading of a computer system.

PCIe Advantages:

Explain why PCIe (PCI Express) is commonly used for high-performance peripherals, outlining its advantages over traditional PCI slots.

Section 2:

Classify and Compare

Chipset Types:

Compare and contrast Northbridge and Southbridge, highlighting the types of components and peripherals each is responsible for managing.

Expansion Slot Types:

Classify PCI, PCIe, and AGP based on their characteristics, use cases, and relevance in modern computer systems.

Section 3:

Practical Application

Upgrading Systems:

Provide a scenario where a user might utilize expansion slots to upgrade their computer system. Mention the type of expansion card(s) they might use and the benefits of this upgrade.

Compatibility Considerations:

Discuss why understanding the compatibility between a motherboard's chipset and expansion cards is crucial before making upgrades. Provide an example scenario.

Section 4:

Critical Thinking

Future of Expansion Slots:

Share your perspective on the future of expansion slots. Do you think they will remain relevant in upcoming computer architectures? Justify your opinion.

Impact of Chipset Design:

Discuss how a well-designed chipset can impact not only system performance but also the overall user experience. Provide examples or real-world implications.

Section 5: Reflection

Personal Experience:

Reflect on a personal experience where understanding chipset architecture and expansion slots played a crucial role in a computer-related decision or issue resolution.

BIOS Setup Utility Quiz and Assignments

Exploring BIOS Setup Utility

Section 1:

True or False

The BIOS Setup Utility allows users to modify system hardware settings and configurations.

True / False

To access the BIOS Setup Utility, users press a specific key during the operating system's loading phase.

True / False

UEFI is an older system interface, and modern systems no longer use it.

True / False

The BIOS Setup Utility provides information about the computer system, including BIOS version and CPU details.

True / False

Users can configure hardware settings, security features, and advanced configurations within the BIOS Setup Utility.

True / False

Section 2:

Multiple Choice

How can users typically access the BIOS Setup Utility?

a) During the operating system's loading phase

b) By pressing a specific key during the system boot-up process

c) Automatically when the computer is powered on

d) Through a shortcut on the desktop

What does UEFI stand for?

a) Universal External Firmware Interface

b) Unified Extensible Firmware Interface

c) Ultra-Fast External Interface

d) User Environment for Firmware Integration

What kind of information does the BIOS Setup Utility provide about the system?

a) Only internet-related details

b) Software and application information

c) System hardware information

d) User login history

Section 3:

Fill in the Blank

The BIOS Setup Utility allows users to customize hardware settings and _____.
Saving changes in the BIOS Setup Utility triggers a _____ to apply the new configurations.

Section 4:
Matching

Match the following:

UEFI Firmware

a) Displays essential system information.

Security Settings

b) Manages system security features.

Advanced Settings

c) Provides a user-friendly interface in modern systems.

Save and Exit

d) Offers additional customization and control.

Section 5:
Short Answer

Explain why it's crucial for users to access the BIOS Setup Utility.

Name two types of information about the system that the BIOS Setup Utility typically displays.

Section 6:
Critical Thinking

Discuss a scenario where adjusting advanced settings in the BIOS might be beneficial.

Why is it important to save changes before exiting the BIOS Setup Utility?

Section 7:
Reflection

Share your experience or thoughts on accessing and using the BIOS Setup Utility.

How might the BIOS Setup Utility contribute to troubleshooting and optimizing a computer system?

Assignment:
Understanding the BIOS Setup Utility
Task 1:
Accessing the BIOS Setup Utility

Explain the process of accessing the BIOS Setup Utility during the system boot-up process. Include the key or keys commonly used for this purpose.

How does accessing the BIOS Setup Utility differ in modern systems with UEFI firmware compared to traditional BIOS systems?

Task 2:

Key Features and Functions

List and briefly describe the essential system information displayed by the BIOS Setup Utility.

Provide examples of hardware configurations that users can modify in the BIOS Setup Utility. Why might users adjust these configurations?

Discuss the significance of security settings offered in the BIOS Setup Utility. Name at least two security features that users can manage through this interface.

Explain the purpose of advanced settings in the BIOS Setup Utility. Provide an example of an advanced configuration that users might customize.

Task 3:

Save and Exit Process

Outline the steps involved in saving changes and exiting the BIOS Setup Utility. Why is it important to follow this process?

Discuss the potential impact of not saving changes before exiting the BIOS Setup Utility.

Task 4:

Real-world Application

Share a scenario where accessing and modifying settings in the BIOS Setup Utility might be necessary or beneficial. How could this contribute to system customization or troubleshooting?

Task 5:

Reflection

Reflect on the role of the BIOS Setup Utility in the overall computer system. Why is it considered a crucial interface for users, and how does it contribute to system management?

Submission Guidelines:

Your assignment should be well-organized and clearly written.

Provide concise and relevant information for each task.

Include any personal experiences or insights you may have regarding the BIOS Setup Utility.

Central Processing Unit (CPU) Quiz and Assignments

Quiz:

Understanding the Central Processing Unit (CPU)

1. What is the Central Processing Unit (CPU) often referred to as in a computer system?

a. Heart

b. Brain

c. Nerve

2. What is the primary responsibility of the CPU?

a. Storing data

b. Executing instructions

c. Managing peripherals

3. What does ISA stand for in the context of CPU architecture?

a. Internal Storage Adapter

b. Instruction Set Architecture

c. Integrated System Algorithms

4. How does a CPU's pipeline architecture contribute to processing efficiency?

a. It reduces the number of supported instructions.

b. It divides the instruction execution process into stages.

c. It eliminates the need for instruction decoding.

5. What are the main stages in the instruction pipeline of a CPU?

a. Fetch, Decode, Execute, Writeback

b. Load, Save, Execute, Print

c. Input, Process, Output

6. What does CISC architecture stand for, and what is a characteristic of CISC?

a. Complex Instruction Set Computer; supports a rich set of complex instructions.

b. Centralized Instruction System Core; focuses on simplicity.

c. Common Integrated System Chipset; reduces hardware complexity.

7. What is the focus of RISC architecture, and why is it designed this way?

a. Rich Instruction Set Computer; for diverse computing tasks.

b. Reduced Instruction Set Computer; for optimized performance and reduced complexity.

c. Random Integrated System Chipset; for unpredictable tasks.

8. What is the significance of multi-core and parallel architectures in modern CPUs?

a. They increase power consumption.

b. They reduce processing speed.

c. They enhance performance, concurrency, and multitasking capabilities.

9. How does a multi-core CPU differ from a single-core CPU?

a. Multi-core CPUs have multiple processing cores, allowing for parallel processing.

b. Single-core CPUs have more cache memory.

c. Multi-core CPUs have fewer instructions.

10. What term is commonly used to describe the simultaneous execution of multiple threads and tasks across CPU cores?

a. Multithreading

b. Megaprocessing

c. Miniloading

11. Which architecture, CISC or RISC, is more focused on simplicity and fundamental instructions?

a. CISC

b. RISC

12. What is the role of the instruction set in CPU architecture?

a. It defines the set of instructions, operations, data types, and addressing modes.

b. It manages the CPU's power consumption.

c. It determines the physical size of the CPU.

Assignment:
Exploring the Central Processing Unit (CPU)
Task 1:
Role of the CPU

Explain in simple terms the role of the Central Processing Unit (CPU) in a computer system. Provide examples to illustrate how the CPU functions as the "brain" of the computer.

Task 2:
ISA and CPU Interaction

Define ISA (Instruction Set Architecture) and describe how it influences the interaction between software applications, operating systems, and the CPU. Use straightforward language to explain why ISA is crucial for seamless communication.

Task 3:
CPU Pipeline Architecture

Illustrate the concept of CPU pipeline architecture. Break down the stages (fetch, decode, execute, writeback) and explain how this architecture enhances processing efficiency. Provide a real-world analogy to make it more relatable.

Task 4:
CISC vs. RISC

Compare CISC (Complex Instruction Set Computer) and RISC (Reduced Instruction Set Computer) architectures. Highlight the key differences between them, emphasizing their impact on complexity, power consumption, and execution times.

Task 5:
Multi-core and Parallel Architectures

Explore the idea of multi-core and parallel architectures in modern CPUs. Explain how these architectures improve performance, concurrency, and multitasking. Use simple examples to illustrate the benefits of having multiple CPU cores.

Task 6:

Real-world Application

Discuss a real-world application or scenario where understanding CPU architecture is crucial. This could be related to everyday technology use or a specific industry. Explain how the choice of CPU architecture can influence performance in this context.

Task 7:

Personal Reflection

Share your thoughts on why understanding the CPU's role and architecture is essential in today's technology-driven world. Discuss any personal experiences or observations that highlight the significance of the CPU in your daily life.

CPU Cooling and Thermal Management Quiz and Assignments

Quiz:

CPU Cooling and Thermal Management

1. What is the primary purpose of CPU cooling and thermal management?

a. Increase CPU clock speed

b. Prevent overheating and optimize CPU performance

c. Enhance gaming experience

d. Extend the lifespan of the motherboard

2. Why does a CPU generate heat during operation?

a. Due to the color of the CPU

b. Energy consumed during tasks and electrical resistance in components

c. Random occurrence

d. Inherent property of the CPU

3. What is thermal throttling, and why is it implemented?

a. Increasing CPU temperature intentionally

b. Reducing performance to prevent overheating

c. Enhancing gaming performance

d. Boosting clock speeds for better speed

4. What is the function of a heat sink in CPU cooling?

a. Increase CPU temperature

b. Dissipate heat from the CPU

c. Generate airflow

d. Store excess heat

5. How does liquid cooling differ from air cooling in CPU systems?

a. Liquid cooling uses fans, while air cooling uses liquid-filled tubes

b. Liquid cooling is always more affordable

c. Air cooling involves closed-loop systems

d. Liquid cooling transfers heat to a radiator through liquid-filled tubes

6. What is the purpose of thermal paste in CPU cooling?

a. Adds color to the CPU

b. Enhances thermal conductivity and fills microscopic gaps

c. Acts as a CPU fan

d. Increases CPU clock speed

7. How does the size of a cooler, including the heat sink and fan, affect cooling performance?

a. Larger coolers always provide better cooling

b. Smaller coolers are more efficient

c. Size doesn't impact cooling

d. It depends on the CPU's color

8. What can users do to contribute to optimal airflow within a computer case?

a. Add more thermal paste

b. Place the computer in direct sunlight

c. Proper cable management, case fan placement, and clean air filters

d. Increase ambient temperature

9. What role does ambient temperature play in CPU cooling efficiency?

a. No impact on cooling efficiency

b. Reduces the risk of leaks in liquid cooling systems

c. Increases overall effectiveness of cooling solutions

d. Causes thermal throttling

10. How can users monitor CPU temperatures?

a. Only through direct observation of the CPU

b. Use monitoring software or check values in BIOS/UEFI

c. Check the color of the CPU

d. Rely on liquid cooling systems

11. Why do CPUs employ thermal throttling?

a. To increase clock speeds

b. To boost gaming performance

c. To reduce performance when temperatures are too high

d. To enhance the color of the CPU

12. What is the purpose of fan speed control in thermal management?

a. Increase fan noise for a better experience

b. Maintain a constant fan speed

c. Adjust fan speeds based on temperature for balanced performance

d. Keep fans at maximum speed at all times

Assignment:
CPU Cooling and Thermal Management

1. Essay Question:

Explain the importance of efficient CPU cooling in computer hardware design. Discuss the potential consequences of inadequate cooling on CPU performance and longevity.

2. Practical Application:

Research and identify a popular air cooling solution for CPUs. Provide details on its design, features, and user reviews. Discuss how this cooling solution contributes to effective thermal management.

3. Critical Thinking:

Compare and contrast air cooling and liquid cooling methods for CPUs. Highlight the advantages and disadvantages of each approach, considering factors such as installation complexity, cost, and cooling efficiency.

4. Case Study:

Investigate a real-world scenario where improper CPU cooling led to system issues or failures. Analyze the case, identify the causes, and propose solutions for preventing similar problems in the future.

5. Practical Demonstration:

Create a step-by-step guide with visuals on the correct application of thermal paste between a CPU and a heat sink. Explain the significance of proper thermal paste application in CPU cooling.

6. Research Paper:

Write a research paper on the factors influencing CPU cooling performance. Explore the impact of cooler design, airflow in the chassis, and ambient temperature on the overall efficiency of CPU cooling solutions.

7. Debate:

Organize a debate discussing the necessity of liquid cooling over air cooling or vice versa. Assign roles to participants advocating for each method and encourage arguments based on cost, performance, and ease of maintenance.

8. Presentation:

Prepare a presentation on the role of temperature monitoring and fan speed control in thermal management. Explain how these features contribute to maintaining optimal CPU temperatures and preventing overheating.

9. Troubleshooting Exercise:

Develop a troubleshooting guide for common CPU cooling issues. Include scenarios such as fan malfunctions, overheating, or inadequate thermal paste application. Provide step-by-step solutions for each problem.

10. Future Trends:

Investigate and speculate on future trends in CPU cooling technology. Discuss potential advancements in materials, designs, or methods that may further improve thermal management in computer systems.

Overclocking Basics Quiz and Assignments

Quizzes on Overclocking Basics

Risk Assessment:

1. What is a potential risk associated with overclocking related to heat generation, and how can it impact CPU stability?
a) Increased data storage
b) Improved system responsiveness
c) Overheating and stability issues

Component Wear:

2. How might excessive overclocking contribute to component wear, and which component is particularly affected?
a) GPU wear, reducing graphics performance
b) Increased wear on RAM modules
c) Wear on CPU components, potentially reducing lifespan

Data Corruption Awareness:

3. Why is finding a stable overclock crucial to avoiding certain undesirable outcomes, such as system crashes or data corruption?
a) Stable overclocks have no impact on system stability.
b) Unstable overclocks can lead to data corruption or system crashes.
c) Data corruption only occurs with default CPU settings.

Performance Boost Recognition:

4. What is a potential reward of overclocking in terms of system performance?
a) Reduced system responsiveness
b) Noticeable performance boost
c) Decreased rendering times

Cost-Efficiency Understanding:

5. How does overclocking contribute to cost-efficiency for users?
a) Increases the need for immediate CPU upgrades
b) Delays the need for hardware upgrades
c) Enhances the need for additional cooling solutions

Personalization Impact:

6. In what way does overclocking allow users to personalize their system's performance?
a) Limits system customization options

b) Balances power and efficiency based on individual preferences

c) Reduces overall system responsiveness

Stress Testing Tools:

7. Name a tool commonly used for stress testing a CPU before overclocking.

a) Microsoft Word

b) Prime95

c) Adobe Photoshop

Temperature Monitoring Importance:

8. Why is monitoring CPU temperature crucial during overclocking?

a) To increase power consumption

b) To enhance system aesthetics

c) To ensure stability and prevent overheating

BIOS/UEFI Adjustments:

10. Which BIOS/UEFI settings are commonly adjusted for overclocking, impacting the CPU clock speed?

a) Adjusting mouse sensitivity

b) Tweaking CPU multiplier and base clock frequency

c) Changing monitor resolution

Voltage Settings Awareness:

11. How can adjusting CPU voltage impact overclocking, and what precaution should be taken?

a) Decreasing voltage to increase stability

b) Increasing voltage without consequences

c) Excessive voltage increases can contribute to higher temperatures and reduce CPU lifespan

Incremental Changes Method:

12. Why is the approach of incrementally increasing clock speeds and voltages recommended during overclocking?

a) It speeds up the overclocking process

b) It avoids stability testing

c) It helps find the optimal balance between performance and stability

Memory Overclocking Purpose:

13. How does overclocking RAM complement CPU overclocking, and what aspects are adjusted for memory overclocking?

a) RAM overclocking has no impact on overall system performance

b) Adjusting memory timings and frequencies can enhance overall system performance

c) Overclocking RAM only affects graphics performance

Cooling Solution Significance:

14. Why is investing in high-quality cooling solutions crucial when overclocking?

a) To increase system cost

b) To make the system heavier

c) Effective cooling is crucial for managing increased heat generated by overclocking

Thermal Paste Application Purpose:

15. What is the purpose of applying thermal paste between the CPU and the cooler in overclocking scenarios?

a) For aesthetic improvement

b) To reduce CPU clock speed

c) For improved heat transfer and stability

Backup System Importance:

16. Why is it advised to have a backup system or data backup before overclocking?

a) Overclocking poses no risk to system stability

b) It's a precautionary measure in case of system instability or data loss

c) Backup systems are not necessary for overclocking

Assignment:
Overclocking Basics
Question 1:
Understanding Risks and Rewards
a. Risks of Overclocking:

Heat Generation: Explain how overclocking increases heat generation in the CPU and the potential consequences if not managed properly.

Component Wear: Describe the long-term impact of overclocking on CPU components and the role of adequate cooling in mitigating wear.

b. Rewards of Overclocking:

Performance Boost: Elaborate on how overclocking can lead to a noticeable performance boost, especially in CPU-intensive tasks.

Cost-Efficiency: Discuss how overclocking contributes to cost-efficiency by maximizing the potential of existing hardware, delaying the need for immediate upgrades.

Personalization: Explain how overclocking allows users to personalize their system's performance based on individual preferences.

Question 2:
Practical Overclocking Techniques
a. Stress Testing and Monitoring:

Stress Testing: Define the purpose of stress testing before overclocking and mention specific tools used for stress testing the CPU.

Temperature Monitoring: Highlight the importance of temperature monitoring during overclocking and its role in maintaining system stability.

b. BIOS/UEFI Settings:

Multiplier and Frequency: Explain the process of adjusting the CPU multiplier and base clock frequency in the BIOS/UEFI for overclocking, emphasizing the need for caution.

Voltage Settings: Discuss the role of adjusting CPU voltage in stabilizing overclocks and the potential consequences of excessive voltage increases.

c. Incremental Changes:

Gradual Overclocking: Describe the strategy of incrementally increasing clock speeds and voltages during overclocking and its impact on finding the optimal balance between performance and stability.

Memory Overclocking: Explain how overclocking RAM complements CPU overclocking and its contribution to overall system performance.

d. Cooling Solutions:

Quality Cooling: Discuss the importance of investing in high-quality cooling solutions for managing increased heat generated by overclocking.

Thermal Paste: Describe the role of applying thermal paste between the CPU and the cooler and its significance in ensuring stable performance under overclocked conditions.

e. Backup and Restore:

BIOS/UEFI Profiles: Explain the purpose of saving multiple profiles in the BIOS/UEFI and how it facilitates quick recovery in case of instability during overclocking.

Backup System: Emphasize the importance of backing up important data before overclocking and why it serves as a precautionary measure.

Memory and Storage Quiz and Assignments

Quizzes on Memory and Storage

1. Types of Memory:

a. RAM (Random Access Memory):

1. What does DDR stand for in DDR SDRAM?

A. Double Data Rate

B. Dynamic Data Retrieval

C. Digital Data Rendering

D. Data Duplication Rate

2. Why is DDR SDRAM considered faster than SDR SDRAM?

A. It has a higher storage density.

B. It uses a more complex latching circuitry.

C. It transfers data on both rising and falling edges of the clock signal.

D. It requires less frequent refreshing.

b. SRAM (Static Random Access Memory):

3. What distinguishes SRAM from DRAM in terms of data storage?

A. SRAM uses latching circuitry.

B. SRAM requires constant refreshing.

C. SRAM is non-volatile.

D. SRAM has a slower access speed.

4. Where is SRAM often used in computer systems?

A. Main system memory

B. Hard drives

C. Cache memory in CPUs

D. Graphics cards

c. DRAM (Dynamic Random Access Memory):

5. What is the primary drawback of DRAM compared to SRAM?

A. Higher cost

B. Slower access speed

C. Requires constant refreshing

D. Lower storage density

6. In which computer component is DRAM commonly used?

A. Hard drives

B. CPU cache

C. Main system memory

D. Graphics cards

2. ROM (Read-Only Memory):
a. Types of ROM:

7. What does EPROM stand for?

A. Electrically Erasable Programmable Read-Only Memory

B. Erasable Permanent Read-Only Memory

C. Efficient Programming Read-Only Memory

D. Electronic Permanent Read-Only Memory

8. How is data written onto Mask ROM?

A. Electronically

B. Using ultraviolet light during manufacturing

C. Through constant refreshing

D. None of the above

b. Applications of ROM:

9. What is the primary purpose of ROM in a computer system during startup?

A. Storing temporary data

B. Executing application software

C. Storing boot firmware

D. Managing cache memory

10. In which type of systems is ROM commonly used for permanent data storage?

A. Gaming consoles

B. Embedded systems

C. Laptops

D. External hard drives

Assignment on Memory and Storage
1. RAM (Random Access Memory):
a. DDR SDRAM (Double Data Rate Synchronous Dynamic RAM):

1. What does DDR stand for in DDR SDRAM, and how does it differ from SDR SDRAM?

2. Enumerate the characteristics of DDR SDRAM, including different generations and their improvements.

3. Explain why DDR RAM is considered widely used in modern computers and mention its primary tasks.

b. SRAM (Static Random Access Memory):

4. Contrast SRAM with DRAM, emphasizing the key differences in data storage and cost.

5. Discuss the role of SRAM as cache memory in CPUs and its significance for system performance.

c. DRAM (Dynamic Random Access Memory):

6. Highlight the characteristics of DRAM, focusing on cost, access speed, and its role as the main system memory.

7. Explain why DRAM requires constant refreshing and its suitability for high-capacity memory modules.

2. ROM (Read-Only Memory):
a. Types of ROM:

8. Define Mask ROM and explain how permanent data is stored in this type of memory.

9. Differentiate between EPROM and EEPROM, emphasizing the methods used for erasing and reprogramming.

b. Applications of ROM:

10. Discuss the role of ROM in storing boot firmware, especially during the computer's startup process.

11. Explore the common applications of ROM in embedded systems and devices, emphasizing the need for permanent data storage.

General Reflection Question:

12. Why is the distinction between volatile and non-volatile memory important, and how does it impact the functionality of a computer system?

Storage Devices Quiz and Assignments
Quizzes on Storage Devices and RAID Configurations
1. HDDs, SSDs, and Hybrid Drives:
a. HDD (Hard Disk Drive):
1. What is the primary technology used in HDDs to store and retrieve data?
2. Name one disadvantage of HDDs related to their mechanical components.
b. SSD (Solid State Drive):
3. How do SSDs achieve faster data access speeds compared to HDDs?
4. Identify one advantage of SSDs concerning durability.
c. Hybrid Drives (SSHD):
5. What key feature distinguishes hybrid drives from traditional HDDs?
6. In hybrid drives, how does the SSD cache contribute to improved performance?
2. RAID Configurations:
a. RAID (Redundant Array of Independent Disks):
7. What does RAID stand for, and what is its primary purpose?
8. Explain the key characteristic of RAID 0 regarding data redundancy.
b. Common RAID Configurations:
9. In RAID 1, what is the main advantage concerning data protection?
10. Why is RAID 5 considered a balance between performance and redundancy?
11. Describe the combination of features in RAID 10 and its benefits.
c. Applications and Implementation:
12. Where are RAID configurations commonly used to enhance storage performance?
13. Name two methods for implementing RAID – hardware and _____?
General Understanding:
14. Which storage device type (HDD, SSD, or Hybrid) is generally more cost-effective in terms of price per gigabyte?
15. Why are SSDs considered more durable than HDDs?
Reflection Questions:
16. How does the absence of moving parts contribute to the advantages of SSDs?
17. In what scenarios would a Hybrid Drive be a suitable choice compared to standalone HDDs or SSDs?
Application of Knowledge:
18. If you were building a high-performance gaming PC, would you choose an HDD, SSD, or Hybrid Drive? Justify your choice.

19. Discuss one real-world scenario where implementing RAID could be highly beneficial.

Critical Thinking:

20. Considering the advantages and disadvantages, propose a situation where you might prefer an HDD over an SSD or vice versa.

Assignments on Storage Devices and RAID Configurations
Assignment 1:
Storage Devices

1. Explain the main components of an HDD and why it is considered more susceptible to mechanical failure compared to SSDs.

2. List three advantages of SSDs over HDDs, highlighting the impact of having no moving parts.

3. If you were building a budget-friendly computer for storing large files, would you choose an HDD or SSD? Justify your choice.

4. Describe the key feature of Hybrid Drives that allows them to balance both capacity and performance.

5. Discuss the significance of energy efficiency in SSDs and its implications for portable devices like laptops.

Assignment 2:
RAID Configurations

6. Provide a brief overview of RAID and explain its primary purposes in combining multiple drives.

7. Compare and contrast the advantages and disadvantages of RAID 0 and RAID 1.

8. In what scenarios would RAID 5 be a suitable choice, considering its balance between performance and fault tolerance?

9. Explain the concept of RAID 10, highlighting its combination of features and requirements.

10. Discuss two applications where RAID configurations are crucial for enhancing storage performance and reliability.

Reflection and Application:

11. Reflect on the importance of automatic data management in Hybrid Drives. How does it contribute to overall system performance?

12. Imagine you are a system administrator responsible for a server in an enterprise environment. Would you choose hardware controllers or software-based solutions for implementing RAID? Justify your choice.

13. Connect the knowledge of SSDs and RAID configurations. How might using SSDs impact the performance of a RAID setup?

Critical Thinking:

14. Consider the evolution of storage devices. In what ways have advancements in SSD technology influenced the industry's approach to traditional HDDs?

15. Discuss the potential risks associated with relying solely on RAID configurations for data protection. What additional measures might be necessary?

Real-World Application:

16. Research and provide an example of a specific industry or business that heavily relies on RAID configurations for its daily operations. Explain the reasons behind their choice.

Group Discussion:

17. In a group discussion, explore the future trends in storage technologies. How might developments in storage impact everyday computing and business operations?

Practical Scenario:

18. Assume you are advising a small business owner on setting up a storage solution. Based on their needs (considering factors like cost, performance, and reliability), recommend a suitable combination of storage devices and RAID configurations. Justify your recommendations.

Storage Interfaces Quiz and Assignments

Quizzes on Storage Interfaces

SATA (Serial ATA):

1. What does SATA stand for, and what is its primary use in a computer system?

2. Name the most common version of SATA and mention its maximum data transfer speed.

3. Explain the backward compatibility feature of SATA and its significance.

NVMe (Non-Volatile Memory Express):

4. Define NVMe and specify the type of storage devices it is designed for.

5. Compare the data transfer speeds of NVMe and SATA, highlighting the advantage of NVMe.

6. What is the M.2 form factor, and why is it commonly associated with NVMe SSDs?

PCIe (Peripheral Component Interconnect Express):

7. Briefly describe the role of PCIe in a computer system and the types of components it connects.

8. How does PCIe achieve scalable bandwidth, and why is this feature important for modern applications?

9. Explain the versatility of PCIe slots and provide an example of a component commonly connected to them.

USB (Universal Serial Bus):

10. Outline the purpose of USB in connecting external devices to computers.

11. Name two versions of USB and describe their differences in terms of data transfer speeds.

12. Highlight the convenience offered by USB's plug-and-play functionality.

General Understanding:

13. If you have an external SSD, would you connect it using a SATA or USB interface for faster performance? Justify your choice.

14. In what scenarios would the backward compatibility of SATA be particularly useful for users?

Compatibility and Connectivity:

15. How does the M.2 form factor contribute to the design of modern, compact laptops or desktops?

16. Discuss one advantage of USB interfaces related to their ability to provide power to connected devices.

Real-World Application:

17. Research and provide an example of a device that typically uses a PCIe slot for improved performance.

Scalability and Performance:

18. Imagine you are building a gaming PC. Explain why you might prioritize components that utilize PCIe interfaces for better gaming performance.

Comparative Analysis:

19. Compare the advantages of NVMe SSDs over traditional SATA SSDs, considering factors like speed and latency.

Future Trends:

20. Predict how the increasing demand for high-speed data transfer in future applications might influence the development of storage interfaces.

Storage Interfaces Assignments
SATA (Serial ATA):

1. Explain the primary purpose of SATA in connecting storage devices to a computer.

2. List the different versions of SATA, and describe the data transfer speed of SATA III. Question: Why is backward compatibility essential in SATA, and how does it benefit users?

NVMe (Non-Volatile Memory Express):

3. Define NVMe and identify the type of storage devices it is designed for.

4. Compare the data transfer speeds of NVMe and SATA, emphasizing the advantages of NVMe.

5. What is the significance of the M.2 form factor in NVMe SSDs, and how does it contribute to their design?

PCIe (Peripheral Component Interconnect Express):

6. Describe the role of PCIe in a computer system and name the components it connects.

7. How does PCIe achieve scalable bandwidth, and why is this important for modern applications?

8. Discuss the versatility of PCIe slots and provide an example of a commonly connected component.

USB (Universal Serial Bus):

9. Outline the primary purpose of USB in connecting devices to computers.

10. Name two USB versions and explain the differences in data transfer speeds.

11. Elaborate on the plug-and-play functionality of USB and its significance for users.

Compatibility and Connectivity:

12. Explain how the M.2 form factor in NVMe SSDs contributes to the design of compact laptops.

13. Discuss one advantage of USB interfaces related to their ability to provide power to connected devices.

Real-World Application:

14. Research and provide an example of a device that typically uses a PCIe slot for enhanced performance.

Scalability and Performance:

15. Imagine you are building a gaming PC. Explain why prioritizing components that utilize PCIe interfaces can contribute to better gaming performance.

Comparative Analysis:

16. Compare the advantages of NVMe SSDs over traditional SATA SSDs, considering factors like speed and latency.

Future Trends:

17. Predict how the increasing demand for high-speed data transfer in future applications might influence the development of storage interfaces.

Keyboards and Mice Quiz and Assignments

Keyboards and Mice Quizzes
Mechanical vs. Membrane Keyboards:
Mechanical Keyboards:

1. What provides the distinctive tactile feel and audible click in mechanical keyboards?

2. Why are mechanical keyboards known for their durability?

Membrane Keyboards:

3. What technology do membrane keyboards use to register key presses?

4. Name one advantage of membrane keyboards related to their operation in quiet environments.

Comparison:

5. What typing experience do mechanical keyboards offer, and who might prefer them?

6. In what scenarios might membrane keyboards be a suitable and cost-effective choice?

Gaming Mice and DPI:

Gaming Mice:

7. What features are gaming mice designed to enhance?

8. Why is the ergonomic design of gaming mice important for users?

DPI (Dots Per Inch):

9. Define DPI and its role in mouse sensitivity.

10. How does adjustable DPI contribute to the versatility of gaming mice?

Comparison:

11. Why do gamers favor gaming mice with higher DPI settings?

12. Besides gaming, how can users benefit from the features of gaming mice in regular computer tasks?

Application and Customization:

Customization of Mechanical Keyboards:

13. Name one aspect of mechanical keyboards that users can customize, and why is it beneficial?

Programmable Buttons on Gaming Mice:

14. How do programmable buttons on gaming mice enhance the gaming experience?

Use Cases and Preferences:

Gaming Keyboard Choice:

15. Explain why a gamer might choose a mechanical keyboard over a membrane keyboard.

Mouse Sensitivity in Graphic Design:

16. In graphic design, why might a user prefer a mouse with higher DPI settings?

Ergonomics and Comfort:

Ergonomic Benefits of Mechanical Keyboards:

17. How does the tactile feedback in mechanical keyboards contribute to user comfort?

Comfort in Prolonged Use:

18. Why is the ergonomic design of gaming mice particularly important for users during long gaming sessions?

Technical Understanding:

Switch Types in Mechanical Keyboards:

19. Briefly explain the difference between linear, tactile, and clicky switches in mechanical keyboards.

Precision in Cursor Movements:

20. How does higher DPI contribute to the precision of cursor movements in gaming mice?

Affordability and Budget Consideration:

Budget-Friendly Keyboard Choice:

21. In what situations might a user opt for a membrane keyboard due to budget considerations?

Cost-Effective Gaming Mouse:

22. How can users find a cost-effective gaming mouse that still offers essential gaming features?

Versatility in Different Environments:

Quiet Operation in Membrane Keyboards:

23. Name one scenario where the quiet operation of a membrane keyboard would be advantageous.

Adaptability of Gaming Mice:

24. How can the adjustable DPI settings on gaming mice adapt to different gaming scenarios?

Future Trends and Technological Advancements:

Future Trends in Keyboards:

25. Predict one possible future trend or technological advancement in keyboard design.

Enhancements in Gaming Mice:

26. Imagine a future enhancement in gaming mice technology. How might it further improve the gaming experience?

Assignments:
Keyboards and Mice
Assignment 1:
Keyboard Preferences
Questions:
Task 1:

Interview three people and ask them about their keyboard preferences.

1. Do you prefer a mechanical or membrane keyboard, and why?
2. How important is keyboard customization to you?

3. In what situations do you find a mechanical keyboard more advantageous than a membrane keyboard?

Task 2:

Research and compile a list of three popular mechanical keyboards and three popular membrane keyboards, including their key features and prices.

Mechanical Keyboards:

Provide information on tactile feedback, durability, and customization options.

Membrane Keyboards:

Highlight features like quiet operation, cost, and keystroke feel.

Assignment 2:

Gaming Mice Analysis

Questions:

3. Task:

Create a comparative analysis between two gaming mice, focusing on their DPI, programmable buttons, and ergonomic design.

Gaming Mouse 1:

Provide details on DPI sensitivity, programmable buttons, and ergonomic features.

Gaming Mouse 2:

Offer similar details for comparison.

Task:

Write a short guide on how to customize DPI settings on a gaming mouse using software. Include screenshots if possible.

Steps:

Outline the steps users need to follow to adjust DPI settings.

Benefits:

Explain the advantages of customizing DPI for different scenarios.

Assignment 3:

Use Cases and Recommendations

Questions:

5. Task:

Identify specific use cases where a mechanical keyboard would be the preferred choice, and provide reasons.

Example:

Suggest scenarios like gaming, programming, or professional typing tasks.

Task:

Recommend a gaming mouse for a user who prioritizes precise cursor movements and quick response times.

Requirements:

Consider factors like DPI, programable buttons, and ergonomic design.

Assignment 4:
Real-World Application
Questions:
7. Task:

Imagine you are a gamer who participates in both competitive and casual gaming. Describe your ideal keyboard and mouse setup, explaining the reasons behind your choices.

Keyboard:

Specify whether you'd choose mechanical or membrane and why.

Mouse:

Detail your preferred DPI sensitivity, button customization, and ergonomic features.

Task:

Write a short paragraph on how the use of gaming mice in professional esports can impact player performance.

Factors:

Consider aspects like DPI precision, programmable buttons, and overall comfort.

Assignment 5:
Technological Trends
Questions:
9. Task:

Research and predict one potential technological trend in keyboard design for the next five years.

Explanation:

Provide reasons for the expected trend and its potential impact.

Task:

Discuss how advancements in gaming mouse technology, such as improved DPI or sensor technology, could influence the gaming industry.

Implications:

Consider how these advancements might affect game development and competitive gaming.

Monitors and Displays Quiz and Assignments

Quizzes on Monitors and Displays
Display Types: LED, LCD, OLED
a. LED (Light-Emitting Diode):

1. What does LED stand for in display technology?

2. Name one advantage of LED displays related to their design.

b. LCD (Liquid Crystal Display):

3. What technology do LCD displays use to create images?

4. Why are LCD monitors considered more affordable than OLED displays?

c. OLED (Organic Light-Emitting Diode):

5. Describe a characteristic feature of OLED displays that contributes to vibrant colors.

6. What is a potential drawback of OLED displays regarding burn-in?

Refresh Rates and Resolution
a. Refresh Rates:

7. How is refresh rate measured, and what unit is used?

8. Why do gamers often prefer monitors with higher refresh rates?

b. Resolution:

9. Define resolution in the context of monitors.

10. What advantage does higher resolution offer for productivity tasks?

Comparison: LED, LCD, OLED

11. Which display type is known for achieving true black levels?

12. In terms of durability, which display type is generally more resistant to burn-in?

Contrast Ratio and Viewing Angles

13. What visual enhancement does a higher contrast ratio provide in displays?

14. What is a notable feature of OLED displays related to viewing angles?

Refresh Rates and Gaming Performance

15. How does a higher refresh rate contribute to smoother motion in displays?

16. Why do gamers often prioritize monitors with refresh rates higher than 60Hz?

Resolution and Image Clarity

17. How is image clarity improved with higher resolutions?

18. Name a scenario where higher resolutions may be particularly beneficial.

Balance in Display Features

19. In what situations is a monitor with a balance of high refresh rates and resolutions beneficial?

20. Why are monitors with balanced features popular among users seeking versatility in their displays?

Assignments on Monitors and Displays

Display Types: LED, LCD, OLED

a. LED (Light-Emitting Diode):

Assignment 1:

List two advantages of LED displays in terms of energy efficiency.

Assignment 2:

Explain how LED technology contributes to slim and lightweight display designs.

b. LCD (Liquid Crystal Display):

Assignment 3:

Describe the role of liquid crystal technology in LCD displays.

Assignment 4:

Discuss why LCD monitors are considered more affordable compared to OLED displays.

c. OLED (Organic Light-Emitting Diode):

Assignment 5:

Define the term "Perfect Blacks" and explain its significance in OLED displays.

Assignment 6:

Highlight one feature of OLED technology that allows for thin and flexible display designs.

Comparison:

Display Types

Assignment 7:

Contrast the contrast ratio of OLED displays with LED and LCD displays.

Assignment 8:

Discuss the potential durability concerns associated with OLED displays, especially in terms of burn-in.

Refresh Rates and Resolution

a. Refresh Rates:

Assignment 9:

Explain how higher refresh rates contribute to smoother motion in displays.

Assignment 10:

Discuss why a refresh rate of 60Hz is considered standard for most monitors.

b. Resolution:

Assignment 11:

Define resolution and its impact on image clarity in monitors.

Assignment 12:

Enumerate the advantages of higher resolutions for productivity tasks.

Comparison: Refresh Rates and Resolution

13. Explore the importance of high refresh rates in gaming performance.

Assignment 14:

Discuss the benefits of monitors that strike a balance between high refresh rates and resolutions.

Audio Devices Quiz and Assignments

Quizzes on Audio Devices

Sound Cards:

1. What is the primary function of a sound card in a computer system?

2. Differentiate between integrated audio and dedicated sound cards.

3. Why might audiophiles choose dedicated sound cards over integrated solutions?

Headphones, Speakers, and Microphones:

4. Describe the main types of headphones and their differences in terms of design and sound isolation.

5. Explain the concept of impedance in headphones and its significance.

6. What is the purpose of speakers, and how do they differ based on configuration (e.g., 2.0, 2.1, 5.1)?

7. Name two types of microphones and specify situations where each is commonly used.

Additional Considerations:

8. What are the advantages of wireless audio devices over wired ones?

9. In the context of gaming audio, mention one feature commonly found in gaming-focused headphones.

10. How does a microphone with omnidirectional capability differ from a directional microphone?

Audio Terminology:

11. Define "impedance" in the context of headphones.

12. What does the term "signal-to-noise ratio" refer to in the context of sound cards?

13. Explain the purpose of a line-in port on a sound card.

Usage and Connectivity:

14. In what scenarios might a content creator prefer using dedicated sound cards?

15. How does the type of headphone (over-ear, on-ear, in-ear) affect comfort and sound isolation?

16. Describe the difference between USB and analog connections for microphones.

Wireless vs. Wired:

17. List one advantage and one disadvantage of using wireless headphones.

18. When might someone choose wired speakers over wireless ones?

Gaming Audio:

19. Name one feature that enhances the gaming experience in headphones designed for gaming.

20. How does a subwoofer contribute to the audio experience in a 2.1 speaker system?

Assignments on Audio Devices

Understanding Sound Cards:

1. Explain the role of sound cards in processing audio signals and their significance in a computer system.

2. Differentiate between integrated audio and dedicated sound cards, highlighting the advantages of each.

Exploring Headphones, Speakers, and Microphones:

3. Define the main types of headphones and discuss the differences in comfort and sound isolation among over-ear, on-ear, and in-ear designs.

4. Describe the types of speakers available and their suitability for different setups. Include configurations such as stereo, 2.1, and multi-channel systems.

5. Provide an overview of the various types of microphones, their applications, and the importance of directionality.

Audio Terminology and Considerations:

6. Define the term "impedance" as it relates to headphones and explain its impact on audio performance.

7. Discuss the factors influencing the choice between wired and wireless options for headphones, speakers, and microphones.

Wireless vs. Wired and Gaming Audio:

8. List one advantage and one disadvantage of using wireless audio devices, considering headphones, speakers, and microphones.

9. Explain the features commonly found in gaming-focused headphones and their significance for an immersive gaming experience.

Integration and Connectivity:

10. Elaborate on the connectivity options provided by sound cards, including the significance of line-out, line-in, and headphone jacks.

11. Discuss how some microphones are integrated into headphones and their practical use for hands-free communication.

Audio Quality and User Preferences:

12. Compare the audio quality offered by integrated audio solutions on motherboards with that of dedicated sound cards.

13. Considering user preferences, discuss the scenarios in which audiophiles or content creators might choose dedicated sound cards.

Expansion Cards and Connectivity Quiz and Assignments
Quizzes on GPU Architecture and SLI/CrossFire Technologies
GPU Architecture Basics:
1. What does GPU architecture refer to, and how does it impact the performance of a graphics card?
2. Name one feature introduced in the Turing architecture by NVIDIA and its significance for realistic graphics.
NVIDIA GPU Architectures:
3. Which GPU architecture introduced real-time ray tracing to NVIDIA graphics cards, and in what year was it released?
4. List two features associated with the Ampere architecture in NVIDIA's RTX 30 Series GPUs.
AMD GPU Architectures:
5. What does GCN stand for in AMD GPU architectures, and what was its primary focus?
6. Highlight one feature introduced in RDNA 2 architecture, as seen in AMD's RX 6000 Series GPUs.
SLI and CrossFire Technologies Overview:
7. Define SLI and CrossFire technologies and explain their purpose in the context of graphics cards.
8. What is the primary goal of connecting multiple GPUs using SLI or CrossFire?
SLI (NVIDIA) and CrossFire (AMD) Configuration:
9. How are two or more NVIDIA GPUs connected in an SLI configuration, and what is the purpose of the SLI bridge?

10. Explain the configuration process for CrossFire, detailing how multiple AMD GPUs collaborate for improved graphics performance.

Performance Considerations:

11. Why might the performance gains from adding a second GPU through SLI or CrossFire not always be proportional to the cost?

12. How does game and application support influence the effectiveness of SLI and CrossFire technologies?

GPU Multi-GPU Configurations:

13. Provide one advantage and one disadvantage of using multi-GPU configurations for gaming and graphics performance.

14. In what scenarios might the use of SLI or CrossFire be less practical or effective?

Advanced GPU Features:

15. Name one feature introduced in RDNA architecture by AMD that aimed to improve gaming performance.

16. What is the significance of Tensor cores in NVIDIA's Turing architecture, especially in relation to AI-based features?

GPU Technology Compatibility:

17. Why is it important to consider software optimization and game support when deciding to use SLI or CrossFire?

18. How can the compatibility of SLI and CrossFire technologies influence a user's decision to invest in multiple GPUs?

Future GPU Developments:

19. Considering recent GPU architectures, name one advancement or feature you would like to see in future graphics cards.

20. Discuss the potential impact of technologies like real-time ray tracing on the future of GPU architecture and gaming experiences.

Assignment on GPU Architectures and Multi-GPU Technologies
Section 1:
GPU Architectures
Understanding NVIDIA GPU Architectures:

1. Explain the key features of the Pascal architecture, focusing on improvements brought to performance and power efficiency.

2. Compare the advancements introduced by Turing and Ampere architectures, emphasizing the significance of real-time ray tracing and AI-based features.

Exploring AMD GPU Architectures:

3. Define the purpose of GCN architecture in AMD GPUs and outline its notable features, including its approach to parallel processing power.

4. Discuss the objectives of RDNA architecture, its improvements over GCN, and how it contributes to gaming performance and efficiency.

Analyzing RDNA 2 Architecture:

5. Provide an overview of RDNA 2, as featured in the RX 6000 Series GPUs, highlighting advancements in ray tracing and overall performance.

6. Explain the specific features of RDNA 2, such as Ray Accelerators, Infinity Cache, and support for DirectX 12 Ultimate.

Section 2:
Multi-GPU Technologies
Understanding SLI (NVIDIA):

7. Define SLI and describe the configuration process where multiple NVIDIA GPUs are connected. Include the role of the SLI bridge.

8. Discuss the intended performance improvement of SLI and the factors influencing its compatibility with games and applications.

Insight into CrossFire (AMD):

8. Explain the configuration of CrossFire and how it enables collaboration between two or more AMD GPUs to enhance graphics performance.

9. Highlight the similarities between SLI and CrossFire in terms of their goals and potential challenges related to game and application support.

Section 3:
Considerations and Reflection
Diminishing Returns in Multi-GPU Setups:

10. Define the concept of diminishing returns in the context of SLI and CrossFire technologies, exploring why the scaling might not be linear.

11. Discuss whether the performance gains achieved through multi-GPU setups justify the cost and potential challenges.

Game Support and Optimization:

12. Investigate the role of game and application support in the effectiveness of SLI and CrossFire, considering the varying levels of optimization in newer titles.

13. Reflect on the implications for users when considering multi-GPU configurations, especially in light of evolving gaming trends and technologies.

Network Cards and Connectivity Quiz and Assignments
Quiz on Network Cards and Connectivity
1. Wired vs. Wireless Networking:
Multiple Choice:

1. What is a key advantage of wired networking over wireless?

A. Greater convenience

B. Higher data transfer speeds

C. Enhanced mobility

D. Easier installation

2. In which situation is wireless networking more suitable?

A. Online gaming

B. Desktop computers

C. Bandwidth-intensive tasks

D. Mobile devices

3. Why are wired networks often considered more secure?

A. They use radio waves for communication

B. They are harder to intercept

C. They offer greater mobility

D. They have lower latency

2. Router and Switch Basics:

True or False:

1. Routers connect different networks together, such as a local network and the internet.

2. Switches forward data to all devices within a local network, causing network congestion.

Fill in the Blank:

3. A router uses [NAT] to manage the translation of private IP addresses within a local network to a single public IP address for internet communication.

4. Managed switches may offer features like VLANs (Virtual Local Area Networks) for segmenting networks and improving [security].

3. General Connectivity Knowledge:

Multiple Choice:

4. What is the primary function of a network switch?

A. Connect different networks

B. Manage internet communication

C. Facilitate communication within a local network

D. Provide firewall protection

5. Which type of connection is suitable for areas where running cables is challenging?

A. Wired networking

B. Wireless networking

True or False:

3. Wireless networks are generally more reliable than wired connections.

4. A switch creates a network within a specific location by connecting multiple devices like computers, printers, and other networked devices. [True/False]

4. Network Device Roles:

Match the Term:

a. Connects different networks together

A. Router

b. Connects multiple devices within a local network

B. Switch

c. Provides flexibility and convenience in network connections

C. Wireless Networking

5. Role Identification:

Short Answer:

1. Explain the role of Network Address Translation (NAT) in a router.
2. Differentiate between the functions of a router and a switch in a network.

Assignment on Network Cards and Connectivity

1. Wired vs. Wireless Networking:

Answer the following questions:

1. Why are wired connections considered more reliable than wireless connections?
2. In what situations is wireless networking more suitable than wired networking?
3. List two advantages of wired networks in terms of security.

2. Router and Switch Basics:

Short Responses:

4. Explain the function of Network Address Translation (NAT) in a router.
5. How do routers contribute to enhancing network security? Provide an example.
6. Describe the primary function of a switch in a local network.

3. Use Case Comparison:

Compare and Contrast:

Compare the use cases of wired and wireless connections. Highlight the scenarios where each type is preferable and provide reasons for your choices.

4. Role Identification:

Match the Term:

a. Connects different networks together

A. Router

b. Connects multiple devices within a local network

B. Switch

c. Provides flexibility and convenience in network connections

C. Wireless Networking

5. Real-world Application:
Scenario Analysis:
Imagine you are setting up a network in a new office space. Discuss the factors you would consider when deciding between a wired or wireless network. Justify your choice based on the office's requirements.

6. Critical Thinking:
Consideration and Reflection:
a. Do you think the advantages of wireless networks in terms of convenience and mobility outweigh the advantages of wired networks in terms of reliability and speed? Justify your opinion.

b. Discuss a real-world scenario where having both a router and a switch in a network would be beneficial.

Peripheral Connectivity Quiz and Assignments
Peripheral Connectivity Quiz

1. What does USB stand for?

a. Universal Serial Bus

b. Ultra Speedy Bandwidth

c. Unifying System Bridge

2. Which USB connector is reversible and versatile, used in modern devices?

a. USB-A

b. USB-B

c. USB-C

3. What is the primary advantage of USB-C over other USB connectors?

a. Larger size

b. Reversible design

c. Square-shaped connector

4. What feature allows Thunderbolt to connect multiple devices through a single port?

a. Data daisy-chaining

b. Thunderbolt looping

c. Cable consolidation

5. Which interface is commonly used for connecting computers to monitors or TVs for audio and video transmission?

a. Thunderbolt

b. HDMI

c. USB

6. What does HDMI stand for?

a. High-Definition Multimedia Interface

b. Hyper Data Transmission

c. Hybrid Media Integration

7. Which HDMI feature enables devices to be controlled with a single remote?

a. HD Audio Support

b. CEC (Consumer Electronics Control)

c. Video Signal Multiplexing

8. Which USB standard provides faster data transfer speeds?

a. USB 1.0

b. USB 2.0

c. USB 3.0

9. What is the purpose of device drivers?

a. Control hardware devices

b. Enhance internet speed

c. Manage system memory

10. What is the installation process for devices that are plug-and-play?

a. Automatic Installation

b. Manual Installation

c. Custom Installation

11. Which USB connector is commonly found on printers and some older devices?

a. USB-A

b. USB-B

c. USB-C

12. What is the function of Device Manager in Windows?

a. Manage installed software

b. View and manage hardware devices

c. Control system settings

13. What does CEC stand for in HDMI technology?

a. Central Entertainment Control

b. Consumer Electronics Control

c. Cable Extension Connector

14. Which interface combines data transfer, video output, and power delivery through a single cable?

a. USB

b. Thunderbolt

c. HDMI

15. What does the term "hot-swapping" mean in USB technology?

a. Connecting devices without restarting the computer

b. Swapping USB ports

c. Using USB in hot environments

16. What does daisy-chaining refer to in Thunderbolt technology?

a. Connecting flowers in a chain

b. Connecting multiple devices through a single port

c. Thunderbolt cable management

17. Which HDMI standard supports higher resolutions like 4K and beyond?

a. HDMI 1.0

b. HDMI 2.0

c. HDMI 3.0

18. Why is USB-C considered versatile?

a. It can only be used for charging.

b. It supports various functions, including data transfer and video output.

c. It is only compatible with Apple devices.

19. What should users consider to ensure compatibility when installing device drivers?

a. Device weight

b. Operating system version

c. Internet speed

20. How can users update, uninstall, or roll back drivers in Device Manager?

a. By visiting the device manufacturer's website

b. By using third-party software

c. Through Device Manager in Windows

Answers:

a, 2. c, 3. b, 4. a, 5. b, 6. a, 7. b, 8. c, 9. a, 10. a, 11. b, 12. b, 13. b, 14. b, 15. a, 16. b, 17. b, 18. b, 19. b, 20. c

Assignment:
Peripheral Connectivity
Part 1:
USB, Thunderbolt, and HDMI
USB Knowledge Check:

a. What does USB stand for?

Universal Serial Bus

b. Name the reversible USB connector used in modern devices.

USB-C

c. Which USB type is standard and rectangular?

USB-A

d. Explain the term "hot-swapping" in the context of USB.

Hot-swapping allows devices to be connected or disconnected without restarting the computer.

Thunderbolt Exploration:

a. Who developed the Thunderbolt interface?

Intel in collaboration with Apple

b. What does Thunderbolt combine through a single cable?

Data transfer, video output, and power delivery

c. What is the advantage of Thunderbolt's daisy-chaining feature?

Simplifies cable management by connecting multiple devices through a single port.

HDMI Understanding:

a. Define HDMI.

High-Definition Multimedia Interface

b. What does HDMI support in terms of signals?

Both audio and video signals through a single cable

c. What does CEC stand for in HDMI technology, and what function does it provide?

Consumer Electronics Control;Enables devices to be controlled with a single remote.

Part 2:

Device Drivers and Installation

Device Driver Basics:

a. What is the role of device drivers in a computer system?

Device drivers enable the operating system to communicate with and control hardware devices.

b. Differentiate between automatic and manual installation of device drivers.

Automatic Installation: Operating system installs drivers upon connection.

Manual Installation: Users download and install drivers from the manufacturer's website.

Device Manager Mastery:

a. Where can users access Device Manager in Windows?

Device Manager is a Windows tool accessible through the Control Panel.

b. What functions can users perform in Device Manager regarding device drivers?

Update, uninstall, or roll back drivers.

c. Name an additional consideration when dealing with device drivers.

Ensure drivers are compatible with the operating system version.

d. Why is manufacturer support essential for device drivers?

Manufacturers release updates for improved compatibility and performance.

Power Supplies and Cases Quiz and Assignments

Power Supplies and Cases Quiz:

Understanding Power Supplies:

Wattage Wisdom:

1. What does wattage represent in a power supply unit (PSU)?

Answer: The amount of power the PSU can deliver to computer components, measured in watts.

2. What factors should be considered when selecting the wattage for a PSU?

Answer: Consider the power needs of components like CPU, GPU, drives, and peripherals. Plan for future upgrades with a slightly higher wattage for stability.

Efficiency Exploration:

3. Define efficiency in the context of power supplies.

Answer: Efficiency reflects how well a power supply converts electrical input into usable power, expressed as a percentage.

4. Explain the 80 PLUS certification and its different ratings.

Answer: The 80 PLUS certification indicates power supply efficiency, with ratings like 80 PLUS, Bronze, Silver, Gold, Platinum, and Titanium. Higher ratings mean greater efficiency.

5. List two benefits of having a power supply with high efficiency.

Answer: Energy savings, resulting in lower electricity bills, and cooler operation due to less heat generation.

Modular vs. Non-modular Dilemma:

6. What is the main advantage of modular power supplies?

Answer: They allow users to detach and attach cables based on their system's requirements for cleaner cable management.

7. Name one benefit and one consideration of non-modular power supplies.

Answer: Benefit - Affordability. Consideration - Potential challenges in cable management due to fixed cables.

8. Why might users choose a modular power supply despite the higher cost?

Answer: Modular PSUs help maintain a neat and organized interior, optimizing airflow for better cooling.

Power Supplies and Cases Assignments:
Understanding Power Supplies:
Wattage Wizardry:

1. Define wattage in the context of a power supply unit (PSU).

Answer: Wattage represents the amount of power a PSU can deliver to computer components, measured in watts (W).

2. What factors should be considered when selecting the wattage for a PSU?

Answer: Consider the power needs of components like CPU, GPU, drives, and peripherals. Choose a slightly higher wattage for future upgrades and system stability.

Efficiency Excellence:

3. Explain what efficiency means for a power supply and how it is measured.

Answer: Efficiency refers to how well a PSU converts electrical input into usable power, expressed as a percentage. It is measured by ratings such as 80 PLUS, Bronze, Silver, Gold, Platinum, and Titanium.

4. List two benefits of having a power supply with high efficiency.

Answer: High efficiency results in energy savings (lower electricity bills) and cooler operation, contributing to lower system temperatures.

Modular vs. Non-modular Dilemma:
Modular Marvel:

5. What is the main advantage of modular power supplies?

Answer: Modular power supplies allow users to detach and attach cables based on their system's requirements, promoting cleaner cable management.

6. Name one benefit and one consideration of modular power supplies.

Answer: Benefit - Improved cable management. Consideration - They tend to be slightly more expensive than non-modular counterparts.

7. Why might users choose a modular power supply despite the higher cost?

Answer: Modular PSUs help maintain a neat and organized interior, optimize airflow, and contribute to better cooling.

Non-modular Necessity:

8. What is the main advantage of non-modular power supplies?

Answer: Non-modular PSUs are generally more budget-friendly than modular options.

9. Name one consideration for non-modular power supplies.

Answer: Cable management may be more challenging, potentially leading to a messier interior.

10. Why should users carefully plan cable routing for non-modular power supplies?

Answer: To avoid obstructing airflow within the case.

Computer Cases Quiz and Assignments

Computer Cases Quizzes:

Types and Form Factors:

Tower Triumph:

1. What is a tower case, and what are its characteristics?

Answer: A tower case is a vertical, upright case that provides ample space for components, efficient cooling, and easy accessibility.

2. In what sizes are tower cases commonly available?

Answer: Tower cases come in various sizes, including mid-tower and full-tower.

Desktop Delight:

3. Describe a desktop case and its characteristics.

Answer: A desktop case is horizontal, designed to sit on a desk, compact, and suitable for small form factor builds.

4. Why might a user choose a desktop case?

Answer: Desktop cases are ideal for space-conscious users and situations where a compact design is preferred.

Cube Conundrum:

5. What is a cube case, and what sets it apart?

Answer: A cube case has a cube-shaped design, providing a balance between size and component compatibility. It often allows for unique layouts.

6. What builds are cube cases suitable for?

Answer: Cube cases are suitable for various builds, offering a balance between size and component compatibility.

Mini-ITX Marvel:

7. Define a Mini-ITX case and its primary characteristic.

Answer: A Mini-ITX case is designed for the Mini-ITX motherboard form factor, emphasizing a compact build.

8. In what scenarios might a Mini-ITX case be preferred?

Answer: Mini-ITX cases are chosen for small, portable, or HTPC (Home Theater PC) setups.

Form Factors:

ATX Awesomeness:

9. What does ATX stand for, and what is its characteristic?

Answer: ATX stands for Advanced Technology eXtended, and ATX cases offer ample space for components, suitable for standard desktop builds.

10. Why is ATX a common choice for desktop builds?

Answer: ATX cases are prevalent due to their spacious design, accommodating standard desktop builds effectively.

Marvelous Micro-ATX:

11. Define Micro-ATX (mATX) and highlight its characteristic.

Answer: Micro-ATX is a smaller motherboard form factor, and mATX cases are more compact, suitable for smaller builds.

12. What is the advantage of choosing a Micro-ATX case?

Answer: Micro-ATX cases offer a smaller footprint without sacrificing too much component space.

Mini-ITX Magic:

13. What is the Mini-ITX form factor, and what makes it unique?

Answer: Mini-ITX is the smallest standard motherboard form factor, and cases for Mini-ITX builds are compact, suitable for small, space-efficient builds.

14. When might a user opt for a Mini-ITX case?

Answer: Mini-ITX cases are chosen for their compact design, ideal for small builds with limited internal space.

Cable Management:
Airflow Ally:

15. How does proper cable management contribute to improved cooling performance?

Answer: Well-managed cables facilitate better airflow within the case, contributing to improved cooling performance.

16. What is one benefit of improved cooling in a computer case?

Answer: Improved cooling helps maintain lower temperatures, enhancing overall system stability.

Aesthetic Ascendance:

17. Why do neat and organized cables enhance the overall look of a computer build?

Answer: Neat and organized cables contribute to a cleaner and more aesthetically pleasing appearance, showcasing components without cable clutter.

18. In what ways can aesthetics impact the overall user experience of a computer setup?

Answer: Aesthetically pleasing setups can provide a more enjoyable and visually appealing user experience.

Maintenance Mastery:

20. How does proper cable management make component maintenance easier?

Answer: Proper cable management makes it easier to access and replace components, reducing the hassle during upgrades or troubleshooting.

21. What is one aspect of maintenance that can be challenging without good cable management?

Answer: Troubleshooting and upgrading can be challenging without good cable management due to tangled and obstructive cables.

Cable Management Techniques:
Channel Champion:

22. What role do cable routing channels play in cable management?

Answer: Cable routing channels guide and hide cables, promoting a clean and organized interior.

23. Where are cable routing channels commonly found in computer cases?

Answer: Many cases have built-in channels or routing spaces behind the motherboard tray.

Tie and Strap Tactics:

24. How do cable ties and velcro straps contribute to effective cable management?

Answer: Securing cables with ties or straps helps bundle and organize them neatly, reducing clutter.

25. Where can users apply cable ties and velcro straps for optimal cable management?

Answer: Users can apply ties and straps at various points, securing cables along case edges or designated tie-down points.

Modular Marvels:

26. What is the advantage of using modular power supplies in cable management?

Answer: Modular power supplies allow users to connect only the necessary cables, reducing excess clutter inside the case.

27. How does reducing cable clutter contribute to improved airflow?

Answer: With only necessary cables connected, airflow within the case can be optimized, contributing to better cooling.

Comb Craze:

28. What is the purpose of cable combs in cable management?

Answer: Cable combs help align and organize individual cables, especially for power supply and GPU cables.

29. How do cable combs contribute to the visual appeal of a computer build?

Answer: Cable combs help maintain a uniform and organized look, enhancing the visual appeal of the build.

Tips for Effective Cable Management:
Planning Prodigy:

30. Why is it important to plan cable routing before installing components?

Answer: Planning ahead allows users to optimize cable placement, preventing issues during installation.

31. What can happen if cable routing is not planned in advance?

Answer: Poorly planned cable routing can lead to tangled and obstructive cables, hindering component installation and maintenance.

Ties that Bind:

32. How can users secure cables effectively during cable management?
Answer: Users can secure cables using cable ties or velcro straps at various points to prevent tangling and maintain organization.

33. What is the benefit of using reusable velcro straps in cable management?
Answer: Reusable velcro straps allow for adjustments and future changes without the need for new ties.

Grouping Gurus:

34. Why is grouping similar cables together a recommended practice in cable management?
Answer: Grouping cables together creates a cleaner and more organized appearance, reducing visual clutter.

35. How does grouping cables make it easier to trace and manage connections during maintenance?
Answer: Grouping cables makes it easier to identify and trace specific connections, simplifying maintenance and upgrades.

Combing Champions:

36. When is it beneficial to use cable combs in cable management?
Answer: Cable combs are beneficial for maintaining a uniform and organized look, especially for power supply and GPU cables.

37. What visual difference can cable combs make in a computer build?
Answer: Cable combs contribute to a clean and organized appearance, enhancing the overall visual appeal of the build.

Computer Cases - Simple Assignments:
Assignment 1:
Case Selection Analysis

Objective: Evaluate and choose the most suitable computer case for different scenarios.

Scenario 1 - Power User Build:

1. Choose a computer case that would be ideal for a power user with multiple high-performance components.
Criteria: Consider ample space, efficient cooling, and easy accessibility for components.

Scenario 2 - Home Office Setup:

2. Select a computer case suitable for a home office setup with limited desk space.
Criteria: Prioritize a compact design while ensuring it can house essential components.

Scenario 3 - Gaming Rig with Unique Layout:

3. Identify a case for a gaming rig where a unique layout is desired, promoting efficient cooling options.

Criteria: Look for a cube-shaped case that allows for creative layouts and supports effective cooling solutions.

Scenario 4 - Portable HTPC (Home Theater PC):

4. Choose a case suitable for a small, portable HTPC setup.

Criteria: Opt for a Mini-ITX case that emphasizes a compact build, ideal for small and portable configurations.

Assignment 2:
Cable Management Mastery

Objective: Demonstrate understanding and application of effective cable management techniques.

Task 1 - Airflow Optimization:

Objective: Improve airflow within the case for better cooling performance.

Steps: Utilize cable routing channels and secure cables with ties or velcro straps to prevent obstruction of airflow paths.

Task 2 - Aesthetic Enhancement:

Objective: Enhance the overall aesthetics of the build through neat and organized cables.

Steps: Use cable ties and velcro straps to create clean cable bundles, and consider the placement of cables for a visually pleasing appearance.

Task 3 - Maintenance Simplification:

Objective: Make component maintenance easier through effective cable management.

Steps: Plan cable routing to allow easy access to components, securing cables with ties or velcro straps for quick and hassle-free maintenance.

Task 4 - Cable Combing for Uniformity:

Objective: Achieve a uniform and organized look using cable combs.

Steps: Apply cable combs to power supply and GPU cables, aligning them neatly for a polished and cohesive appearance.

Assignment 3:
Planning and Presentation

Objective: Develop a plan for building a computer system with a focus on case selection and cable management.

Build Plan Document:

Components: List the components to be used, including motherboard form factor, power supply type, and cooling solutions.

Case Selection: Justify the chosen case based on the intended use and component requirements.

Cable Management Strategy: Outline the cable management techniques to be employed, emphasizing airflow, aesthetics, and maintenance.

Build Presentation:

Format: Create a visually appealing presentation (slides or document) showcasing the selected case, component layout, and planned cable management.

Key Points: Highlight key points such as case features, reasons for selection, and the impact of cable management on overall system performance.

Assignment 4:

Reflection Essay

Objective: Reflect on the importance of choosing the right computer case and implementing effective cable management.

Introduction:

Discuss: Why is selecting an appropriate computer case crucial for system performance and longevity?

Case Selection Impact:

Reflect: Share insights into how the chosen case can impact component temperature, accessibility, and overall user experience.

Cable Management Significance:

Analyze: Explain the significance of effective cable management in terms of airflow, aesthetics, and maintenance.

Personal Experience:

Share: Reflect on personal experiences with case selection and cable management in building a computer system.

Cooling Systems Quiz and Assignments

Cooling Systems - Quizzes:

Quiz 1:

Case Fans and Airflow

1. What is the primary function of intake fans in a computer case?

a. Expel hot air

b. Bring cool air into the case

c. Both a and b

d. None of the above

2. Where are top fans typically positioned in a computer case?

a. Front panel

b. Side panel

c. Top of the case

d. Bottom of the case

3. What type of airflow management creates positive pressure in a case?

a. More intake fans than exhaust fans

b. More exhaust fans than intake fans

c. Equal number of intake and exhaust fans

d. No fans installed

4. How does negative pressure affect dust accumulation in a computer case?

a. Reduces dust buildup

b. Increases dust buildup

c. Has no effect on dust

d. Blows away dust

5. Why is neat cable management important for airflow?

a. It improves aesthetics only

b. It helps in organizing cables neatly

c. It has no impact on airflow

d. It prevents cables from functioning

Quiz 2:

Liquid Cooling Solutions

6. What does AIO stand for in the context of liquid cooling?

a. All-In-One

b. Advanced Integration Operation

c. Artificial Intelligence Overhaul

d. Acclaimed Invention Organization

7. Which component is not part of an AIO liquid cooler?

a. Pump

b. Radiator

c. Water Block

d. Custom Tubing

8. What is a key advantage of custom liquid cooling setups over AIO coolers?

a. Lower cost

b. Easier installation

c. Superior cooling performance

d. Universal compatibility

9. What does RGB lighting add to liquid cooling setups?

a. Increased power

b. Visual appeal

c. Cooling efficiency

d. Sound enhancement

10. Why might custom liquid cooling require more effort in maintenance?

a. It never requires maintenance

b. More components to check

c. AIO coolers need more maintenance

d. Maintenance is the same for both

Bonus:
General Cooling Knowledge

11. What is the purpose of thermal paste in cooling systems?

a. Enhance RGB lighting

b. Improve cable management

c. Facilitate heat transfer

d. Increase fan speed

12. How does overclocking impact the need for advanced cooling solutions?

a. It reduces the need for cooling

b. It has no effect on cooling

c. It increases the need for efficient cooling

d. It only affects liquid cooling

Assignments on Cooling Systems
Assignment 1:
Case Fans and Airflow

1. Explain the role of intake fans in a computer case and why they are important for maintaining optimal temperatures.

2. Differentiate between positive airflow and negative airflow in a computer case. Discuss the advantages and disadvantages of each.

3. Draw a diagram illustrating the strategic placement of case fans in a computer case for efficient airflow. Label intake, exhaust, top, and side fans.

4. List three tips for managing airflow in a computer case. Explain why each tip is essential for effective cooling.

5. In a paragraph, discuss the impact of clear pathways on airflow management within a computer case. How does unobstructed airflow contribute to cooling efficiency?

Assignment 2:
Liquid Cooling Solutions

6. Compare and contrast AIO liquid coolers with custom liquid cooling setups. Highlight the key differences in installation, components, and performance.

7. Explain the purpose of each component in an AIO liquid cooler - pump, radiator, and water block. How do they work together to cool the CPU?

8. Create a pros and cons list for AIO liquid coolers and custom liquid cooling setups. Consider factors such as installation, performance, and visual appeal.

9. Imagine you are building a high-performance gaming PC. Justify whether you would choose an AIO liquid cooler or a custom liquid cooling setup based on your priorities (cost, performance, aesthetics).

10. Discuss the role of liquid cooling in reducing the noise level in a computer system. How does liquid cooling contribute to a quieter computing experience compared to some air coolers?

General Considerations:

11. Why is cost listed as a consideration for both AIO coolers and custom liquid cooling setups? How does the cost factor impact the choice between the two?

12. Briefly explain the concept of positive pressure and negative pressure in the context of computer case airflow. Discuss the trade-offs associated with each pressure type.

13. Share your thoughts on whether liquid cooling is a necessity for all types of computer builds or if it's more suitable for specific use cases. Justify your perspective.

Troubleshooting and Maintenance Quiz and Assignments

Troubleshooting and Maintenance Quizzes

Quiz 1:

Common Issues and Solutions

1. Your computer is not turning on. What are the three possible causes, and what steps can you take to troubleshoot this issue?

2. If your computer is experiencing slow performance, what are the three potential causes, and how can you address each one?

3. You're facing the "Blue Screen of Death" (BSOD). List three possible reasons for this issue and the corresponding solutions.

4. The monitor displays no image. Identify three possible causes and the steps you can take to fix the problem.

5. You are having internet connection issues. Name three potential causes and the recommended actions to resolve them.

Quiz 2:

Diagnostic Tools and Software

6. What is the purpose of Windows Troubleshooter, and how can you access and utilize it for resolving common issues?

7. Explain the information provided by Task Manager. How can you use Task Manager to improve system performance?

8. What role does Event Viewer play in troubleshooting, and where can you find it on a Windows system?

9. Describe the function of Disk Cleanup. How can you use Disk Cleanup to optimize your computer's storage?

10. If you suspect corrupted system files, what is the command to run System File Checker (SFC), and how can it help resolve issues?

11. Why is it important to run regular antivirus and anti-malware scans on your computer? Name a reliable method for performing these scans.

Quiz 3:
General Troubleshooting Knowledge

12. Explain the concept of positive pressure and negative pressure in the context of computer case airflow. What are the trade-offs associated with each?

13. In troubleshooting, why is it advisable to test with alternative hardware components when possible?

14. How can you prevent issues related to loose cables in a computer system? Why is cable management important?

15. Your computer is running out of disk space. List two tools or methods you can use to identify and free up storage.

16. Your computer is experiencing intermittent freezes. What steps would you take to identify the cause and resolve this issue?

17. What precautionary measures should you take before using diagnostic tools or making changes to your system to avoid data loss or other complications?

18. Why is it recommended to check for driver updates when troubleshooting hardware issues? How can you update drivers on a Windows system?

19. Briefly explain the purpose of restarting the router and modem when dealing with internet connection problems.

20. Your computer's RAM is insufficient for your tasks. How can you determine the type of RAM compatible with your system, and what steps should you take to upgrade it?

Troubleshooting and Maintenance Assignments
Assignment 1:
Troubleshooting Scenarios

1. Your computer is not turning on. Outline the step-by-step process you would follow to identify and solve the issue. Include possible causes and solutions.

2. A user reports slow performance on their computer. Provide a detailed troubleshooting plan, considering potential causes and corresponding solutions.

3. The monitor displays no image. Create a guide for troubleshooting this issue, covering causes related to cables, graphics card, and drivers. Include step-by-step solutions.

4. A user is experiencing internet connection problems. Develop a troubleshooting checklist, covering router and modem issues, network cables, and potential ISP problems.

5. The user encounters the Blue Screen of Death (BSOD). Construct a comprehensive troubleshooting guide, including hardware, memory, and operating system-related causes. Provide clear steps for resolution.

Assignment 2:
Diagnostic Tools Utilization

6. Explain the purpose and application of the Windows Troubleshooter. Provide a step-by-step guide on how a user can access and use it for various issues.

7. Discuss the significance of Task Manager in troubleshooting. Describe how it can be used to identify and address performance-related issues. Include real-world examples.

8. Explore the role of Event Viewer in diagnosing system problems. Provide instructions on accessing Event Viewer, interpreting logs, and taking appropriate actions based on findings.

9. Explain the purpose of Disk Cleanup and its benefits. Create a tutorial on using Disk Cleanup, specifying the types of files it targets and the steps to perform a cleanup.

10. Elaborate on the functionality of System File Checker (SFC). Guide users on how to run SFC via Command Prompt, interpret results, and take corrective actions.

11. Discuss the importance of regular antivirus and anti-malware scans. Provide instructions on running scans using a popular security software, emphasizing both scheduled and manual scans.

Software and Firmware Updates Quiz and Assignments
Software and Firmware Updates Quizzes

1. Why are regular updates important for software and firmware?

a. To slow down system performance

b. To enhance security and protect against threats

c. To reduce compatibility with new technologies

2. What is the significance of creating backups before major updates?

a. It speeds up the update process

b. It safeguards important data in case of issues

c. It prevents the need for updates

3. What is the purpose of BIOS (Basic Input/Output System) updates?

a. Enhance hardware communication

b. Improve internet speed

c. Update graphics drivers

4. When should users check for manual software updates?

a. Never, as all updates are automatic

b. Periodically, as some updates require manual initiation

c. Only during a full moon

5. How can users identify the current BIOS version on their system?

a. Ask a friend who knows about computers

b. Check the motherboard manufacturer's website

c. Look for a sticker on the computer screen

6. What is the role of drivers in a computer system?

a. To make coffee for the user

b. To enable communication between the operating system and hardware

c. To design graphics for software

7. Why might BIOS updates be necessary?

a. To make the computer slower

b. To address compatibility issues with new hardware

c. Only for decorative purposes

8. What should users do before initiating a BIOS update?

a. Share the news on social media

b. Create backups to safeguard important data

c. Unplug all cables from the computer

9. What can updated drivers improve?

a. The color scheme of the desktop

b. Hardware performance

c. The taste of the keyboard

10. Why is it essential to maintain a stable internet connection during the update process?

a. To watch online videos during the update

b. To prevent any updates from being installed

c. To ensure a smooth update process without interruptions

11. Which update process requires manual initiation?

a. BIOS updates

b. Automatic updates

c. Both a and b

12. What information should users check in release notes or update descriptions?

a. Their horoscope

b. Changes and improvements in the update

c. Recipes for dinner

13. What is the primary role of automatic updates?

a. To increase manual work for users

b. To ensure users never receive updates

c. To deliver the latest patches and features without manual intervention

14. What is the main function of the BIOS (Basic Input/Output System)?

a. To control the coffee maker

b. To initialize hardware components during system boot

c. To write poetry

15. What is the purpose of automatic driver updates?

a. To create confusion among users

b. To keep drivers up to date without manual intervention

c. To uninstall all drivers

16. When might BIOS updates include security enhancements?

a. During a full moon

b. Never

c. Sometimes, to address potential vulnerabilities

17. What can users do to ensure compatibility with the latest hardware and technologies?

a. Ignore all updates

b. Keep software and firmware up to date

c. Use outdated hardware only

18. What should users do if they encounter a Blue Screen of Death (BSOD)?

a. Ignore it, as it adds color to the screen

b. Update or reinstall problematic drivers, check for memory issues, or perform a system restore

c. Switch to a different computer

19. In which scenarios might manual software and firmware updates be necessary?

a. Only during leap years

b. When users have nothing else to do

c. When updates require manual initiation or intervention

20. How can users download the latest drivers for hardware components?

a. Write a letter to the manufacturer

b. Visit the manufacturer's website or use automatic driver update tools

c. Pray for the drivers to appear on the computer

Assignments: Software and Firmware Updates
Essay Assignment: The Significance of Software Updates

Write an essay discussing the importance of regular software updates. Highlight the key reasons why users should keep their software up to date, emphasizing aspects such as security, performance, compatibility, and reliability. Provide real-world examples to support your points and conclude with recommendations for users on best practices when it comes to software updates.

Step-by-Step Guide:
Manual Firmware Update Process

Create a step-by-step guide for users on how to perform a manual firmware update. Choose a specific device or hardware component (e.g., a router or printer) and outline the necessary steps for checking for updates, downloading the firmware, and updating the device. Include screenshots and clear instructions to make the process user-friendly.

Infographic:
Best Practices for Software Updates

Design an infographic highlighting the best practices users should follow when updating their software. Include visually appealing elements to represent concepts such as creating backups, checking release notes, and maintaining a stable internet connection. Keep the information concise and easy to understand.

FAQ Document:
Common Questions About BIOS Updates

Develop a frequently asked questions (FAQ) document addressing common queries users might have about BIOS updates. Cover topics such as the importance of BIOS updates, the identification of the current BIOS version, and the steps involved in flashing the BIOS. Provide clear and concise answers to each question.

Presentation:
Importance of Driver Updates in Enhancing Performance

Prepare a presentation on the significance of driver updates in enhancing hardware performance. Include slides on why updated drivers matter, the benefits they bring, and how they contribute to improved compatibility. Use visuals, charts, and examples to make the presentation engaging and informative.

Checklist:
Preparing for a Major Software Update

Develop a checklist that users can follow before initiating a major software update. Include items such as creating backups, checking available storage space, and reviewing system requirements. Organize the checklist in a clear and sequential manner to guide users through the necessary preparations.

Case Study:
The Impact of BIOS Updates on System Stability

Write a case study analyzing the impact of BIOS updates on the stability of a computer system. Explore a real-life scenario where a system faced stability issues, and a BIOS update was implemented to address them. Discuss the outcomes, improvements observed, and any challenges faced during the update process.

User Guide:
Enabling Automatic Driver Updates in Operating Systems

Create a user guide detailing the steps users can take to enable automatic driver updates in their operating systems. Provide instructions for different operating systems (e.g., Windows, macOS, or Linux) and include screenshots to guide users through the process.

Comparison Chart:
AIO (All-in-One) Liquid Coolers vs. Air Coolers

Design a comparison chart contrasting AIO liquid coolers and traditional air coolers for CPU cooling. Include key factors such as installation difficulty, cooling performance, noise levels, and maintenance requirements. Use clear visuals to highlight the differences and help users make informed decisions.

Interactive Tutorial:
Updating Graphics Drivers for Enhanced Gaming

Develop an interactive tutorial or online guide demonstrating how users can update their graphics drivers to enhance gaming performance. Include interactive elements such as clickable buttons, quizzes, or simulations to make the learning experience engaging and informative.

Preventative Maintenance Quiz and Assignments

Quizzes:
Preventative Maintenance

1. Why is cleaning your computer important?

a. To enhance the color of the components.

b. To prevent dust buildup and ensure efficient cooling.

c. To make it smell nice.

d. To charge the battery.

Answer: b. To prevent dust buildup and ensure efficient cooling.

2. What should you use to clean the exterior surfaces of your computer?

a. Harsh chemicals.

b. A soft, lint-free cloth and a gentle cleaner for stubborn stains.

c. Sandpaper.

d. Cooking oil.

Answer: b. A soft, lint-free cloth and a gentle cleaner for stubborn stains.

3. How often should you perform cleaning and dust removal for your computer?

a. Once a year.

b. Every day.

c. Every 3-6 months, or more frequently in a dusty environment.

d. Only when you notice a problem.

Answer: c. Every 3-6 months, or more frequently in a dusty environment.

4. What factors can affect the lifespan of computer components?

a. Dust and heat.

b. Moon phases.

c. Computer age.

d. Component color.

Answer: a. Dust and heat.

5. What is a recommended upgrade for extended component lifespan?

a. Adding more dust.

b. Placing the computer in direct sunlight.

c. Regularly optimizing software.

d. Ignoring cooling solutions.

Answer: c. Regularly optimizing software.

6. Which component may have a finite lifespan and degrade over time?

a. Keyboard.

b. Motherboard.

c. Printer.

d. Hard drive.

Answer: d. Hard drive.

7. Why is it important to ensure a well-ventilated environment for your computer?

a. To save energy.

b. To make it more challenging to find.

c. To reduce strain on components and prevent overheating.

d. To create a cozy atmosphere.

Answer: c. To reduce strain on components and prevent overheating.

8. What should you consider before upgrading your computer components?

a. The color of the components.

b. Whether the computer is on or off.

c. Compatibility with existing components, budget constraints, and performance needs.

d. The number of cables connected.

Answer: c. Compatibility with existing components, budget constraints, and performance needs.

Assignment:
Preventative Maintenance
Task 1:
Cleaning and Dust Removal
a. Importance of Cleaning:
Efficient Cooling:

Explain how dust buildup can obstruct airflow, leading to increased temperatures and potential overheating of components.

System Reliability:

Describe how regular cleaning reduces the risk of hardware failures caused by dust accumulation on sensitive components.

Aesthetics:

Highlight how keeping the computer clean enhances its appearance and makes troubleshooting and maintenance more accessible.

b. Cleaning Process:
Exterior Cleaning:

Provide steps for wiping exterior surfaces with a soft, lint-free cloth. Emphasize the use of a gentle cleaner for stubborn stains and the avoidance of harsh chemicals.

Interior Cleaning:

Outline the process of powering off the computer, disconnecting all cables, and using compressed air to blow out dust from components. Include cautions about delicate components and preventing fans from spinning during cleaning.

Monitor and Peripherals:

Recommend cleaning monitors with appropriate screen cleaning solutions and regularly wiping down peripherals such as keyboards and mice to prevent dust and debris buildup.

Frequency:

Advise performing cleaning every 3-6 months, or more frequently if the environment is dusty.

Task 2:
Component Lifespan and Upgrades
a. Understanding Component Lifespan:
Components with Limited Lifespan:

Identify mechanical components like hard drives and fans that may have a finite lifespan. Mention the degradation of batteries in laptops and some motherboards over time.

Factors Affecting Lifespan:

Explain how excessive heat and intensive usage can shorten the lifespan of components.

b. Upgrades for Extended Lifespan:
Hardware Upgrades:
Recommend upgrading to a solid-state drive (SSD) for improved performance and reliability. Suggest adding more RAM to enhance multitasking capabilities and overall system responsiveness.

Regular Backups:
Stress the importance of regularly backing up important data to prevent loss in case of hardware failure.

Cooling Solutions:
Advise installing additional or more efficient cooling solutions to maintain lower temperatures.

Optimization:
Emphasize the need to periodically optimize software and remove unnecessary programs to reduce strain on components.

Environmental Considerations:
Highlight the importance of placing the computer in a well-ventilated area with minimal dust.

c. Upgrade Considerations:
Compatibility:
Stress the need to ensure that upgrades are compatible with existing components. Budget: Advise planning upgrades based on budget constraints and the cost-effectiveness of extending the system's lifespan.

Performance Needs:
Encourage users to evaluate whether upgrades align with their performance needs and usage patterns.

Advanced Topics and Emerging Trends Quiz and Assignments
Quiz:
Advanced Topics and Emerging Trends
Quantum Computing:
1. What is the fundamental unit of information in quantum computing?
Answer: Quantum Bits (Qubits)
2. How do qubits differ from classical bits in terms of states?
Answer: Qubits can exist in multiple states simultaneously due to superposition.
3. What is entanglement in quantum computing?

Answer: Entanglement refers to the state of qubits being directly related, regardless of physical distance.

Quantum Computing Applications:

4. In which fields can quantum computing make a significant impact?

Answer: Cryptography, optimization, drug discovery, and materials science.

5. What challenges do quantum computers currently face?

Answer: Challenges include maintaining qubit stability and minimizing errors.

Neuromorphic Hardware:

6. What does neuromorphic hardware draw inspiration from?

Answer: The structure and functioning of the human brain's neural networks.

7. What is a key focus of neuromorphic hardware in terms of processing?

Answer: Neuromorphic hardware focuses on parallel processing, allowing multiple operations simultaneously.

Neuromorphic Hardware Applications:

8. In which domains does neuromorphic hardware show efficiency?

Answer: Artificial intelligence (AI) and machine learning tasks, including pattern recognition and sensory processing.

9. What is the advantage of neuromorphic hardware in AI tasks?

Answer: It efficiently handles complex, interconnected data.

Current State of Quantum Computing and Neuromorphic Hardware:

10. What is the current status of quantum computers in terms of development?

Answer: Quantum computers are still in the early stages of development.

11. Why is there growing interest in integrating neuromorphic hardware with AI?

Answer: To enhance the efficiency of AI algorithms as they continue to advance.

Bonus Question:

12. What is the potential significance of quantum computing in the field of cryptography?

Answer: Quantum computing has the potential to break certain cryptographic algorithms, leading to the need for quantum-resistant encryption.

Assignment:
Advanced Topics and Emerging Trends
Quantum Computing:

1. Explain what quantum computing is and how it differs from classical computing.

2. Outline the fundamental principles of quantum computing, including the concept of qubits and entanglement.

3. Discuss potential applications of quantum computing and its significance in fields like cryptography and materials science.

4. Summarize the current challenges faced by quantum computers in terms of development.

Neuromorphic Hardware:

5. Describe how neuromorphic hardware draws inspiration from the human brain's neural networks.

6. Explain the key focus of neuromorphic hardware, particularly its emphasis on parallel processing and efficiency.

7. Detail the components used in neuromorphic systems, such as artificial neurons and synapses, and how they replicate biological neural networks.

8. Applications in AI: Discuss the efficiency of neuromorphic hardware in accelerating AI and machine learning tasks, with a focus on pattern recognition and sensory processing.

Current State and Future Directions:

9. Quantum Computing: Provide insights into the current state of quantum computing, including its development stage, challenges, and the involvement of major companies and research institutions.

10. Neuromorphic Hardware: Explore the current status of neuromorphic hardware research and development, highlighting the active involvement of academic institutions and tech companies.

11. Integration with AI: Discuss the growing interest in integrating neuromorphic hardware with AI and machine learning, considering its potential to enhance algorithm efficiency.

Reflection:

Personal Thoughts: Share your personal thoughts on the revolutionary nature of quantum computing and the promising applications of neuromorphic hardware in advancing artificial intelligence.

Implications: Reflect on the potential implications of these emerging technologies on the future of computing and their impact on various industries.

Bonus Question:

12. How do you envision the integration of quantum computing and neuromorphic hardware shaping the technological landscape in the next decade?

Answer: Provide your insights and predictions regarding the combined influence of quantum computing and neuromorphic hardware on future technologies.

Green Computing Quiz and Assignments

Quizzes: Green Computing

Energy-Efficient Hardware:

1. What is the primary focus of green computing?

a. Maximizing energy consumption

b. Reducing the environmental impact of computing technologies

c. Increasing carbon footprint

d. Enhancing hardware complexity

2. How does Energy Star certification benefit consumers?

a. Identifying products with the highest energy consumption

b. Providing information on environmentally conscious choices

c. Promoting excessive power usage

d. Certifying products with the latest features

E-waste Management:

3. What does the term "e-waste" refer to?

a. Efficient computing technologies

b. Electronic waste or discarded electronic devices

c. Energy-efficient components

d. Environmental regulations for computing

4. What is one benefit of refurbishing and reusing electronic devices?

a. Increasing the generation of e-waste

b. Reducing the lifespan of devices

c. Extending the lifespan of devices

d. Encouraging new manufacturing

General Knowledge:

5. Why is it important to reduce the carbon footprint associated with computing devices?

a. To increase energy consumption

b. To contribute to greenhouse gas emissions

c. To lower overall greenhouse gas emissions

d. To promote excessive energy use

6. What is a circular economy approach in the context of e-waste?

a. Discarding electronic devices without recycling

b. Promoting a linear approach to resource usage

c. Reusing and recycling electronic components to minimize waste

d. Encouraging the rapid disposal of electronic devices

True/False Section:

7. Green computing focuses on maximizing the complexity of computing hardware.

1. True

2. False

8. E-waste management involves promoting awareness but not educating consumers about proper disposal methods.

1. True

2. False

Assignment:
Green Computing
Energy-efficient Hardware:

1. What is the primary focus of green computing?

Answer: Reducing the environmental impact of computing technologies.

Low-power Components:

2. How are manufacturers contributing to energy-efficient hardware?

Answer: By designing and producing hardware components with lower power consumption.

Energy Star Certification:

3. What does the Energy Star certification program identify?

Answer: Energy-efficient products.

Efficient Cooling Solutions:

4. How do improved cooling solutions contribute to green computing?

Answer: They help in reducing overall energy consumption.

Importance and Benefits:

5. What is one benefit of energy-efficient hardware mentioned in the assignment?

Answer: Lowering overall greenhouse gas emissions.

E-waste Management:

6. What does "e-waste" refer to?

Answer: Discarded electronic devices and components.

Growing Challenge:

7. What contributes to the growing amount of e-waste globally?

Answer: The rapid pace of technological advancements.

Recycling Programs:

8. What is one action governments, organizations, and manufacturers are taking for e-waste management?

Answer: Implementing e-waste recycling programs.

Refurbishment and Reuse:

9. How can devices in good condition contribute to e-waste management?

Answer: They can be refurbished and reused, extending their lifespan.

Awareness and Education:

10. What are crucial aspects of effective e-waste management mentioned in the assignment?

Answer: Promoting awareness and educating consumers about proper disposal methods.

Importance and Benefits (E-waste):

11. Why is proper disposal of e-waste important?

Answer: To prevent hazardous materials from harming the environment and human health.

Resource Conservation:

12. What is one way recycling e-waste contributes to sustainability?

Answer: It helps recover valuable resources, including metals.

Circular Economy:

13. What does adopting a circular economy approach in e-waste management encourage?

Answer: The reuse and recycling of electronic components, minimizing waste.

Hands-on Project Quiz and Assignments

Hands-on Project: Quiz Questions

Planning Phase:

1. What is the first step in planning the build and configuration of a computer system?

Answer: Defining the purpose of the computer.

Budgeting:

2. Why is it important to establish a budget for the project?

Answer: To consider the cost of components and stay within financial constraints.

Component Selection (GPU):

3. How should you choose a graphics card (GPU) for your computer system?

Answer: Based on the intended use (e.g., gaming, graphic design).

Building Phase (Static Precautions):

4. What precautionary measures should be taken during the building phase to prevent static electricity damage?

Answer: Work on an anti-static mat or use an anti-static wrist strap.

BIOS Configuration (OS Installation):

5. How can you install the operating system (OS) on your newly built computer system?

Answer: Using a USB drive or installation disc.

Troubleshooting (Boot Issues):

6. What should you check if your computer is experiencing boot issues after assembly?

Answer: Check connections, ensure components are seated properly, and troubleshoot any boot-related problems.

Performance Optimization (BIOS/UEFI Updates):

7. Why should you check for BIOS/UEFI updates on the motherboard manufacturer's website?

Answer: To improve system stability and compatibility.

Temperature Management (Dust Management):

8. What is a crucial aspect of temperature management to prevent overheating?

Answer: Regularly cleaning dust from components.

System Maintenance (Backup Solutions):

9. What is a recommended practice for system maintenance to safeguard important data?

Answer: Implementing a regular backup strategy.

Security Software:

10. What type of software should be installed and updated for system security?

Answer: Antivirus and anti-malware software.

Regular Updates:

11. Why is it important to keep the OS, drivers, and software up to date?

Answer: To benefit from performance improvements and security patches.

Overclocking (Optional):

12. If desired, what can you explore to enhance CPU or GPU performance?

Answer: Overclocking, with caution and temperature monitoring.

Benchmarking:

13. What activity helps assess system performance and identify potential bottlenecks?

Answer: Running benchmarks.

Peripheral Setup:

14. When should you connect peripherals like the monitor, keyboard, and mouse during the building process?

Answer: After securing the motherboard and installing components.

Airflow Assessment:

15. Why is it important to evaluate the case's airflow during temperature management?

Answer: To identify and address potential cooling issues.

Cooling Solutions:

16. What additional components can be considered for temperature optimization?

Answer: Aftermarket CPU coolers or case fans.

Driver Updates:

17. Why should graphics, chipset, and other drivers be updated?

Answer: To ensure optimal performance.

Backup Strategy:

18. How often should a regular backup strategy be implemented?

Answer: As a regular practice, depending on data importance.

Multitasking Needs:

19. How should RAM be chosen during component selection?

Answer: Based on system requirements and multitasking needs.

Efficiency for System Performance:

20. Why is efficiency important for selecting components like fans and heat sinks?

Answer: To contribute to reducing overall energy consumption.

Hands-on Project: Assignments
Assignment 1:
Build Planning (Define Purpose and Budgeting)

1. Why is it essential to determine the primary use of the computer before selecting components?

2. What factors should be considered when establishing a budget for the computer build project?

Assignment 2:
Component Selection

3. How do you choose a CPU for your computer system, and what factors should be considered?

4. In what ways does the intended use (e.g., gaming, graphic design) influence the selection of a GPU?

5. Why is it important to choose RAM based on both system requirements and multitasking needs?

Assignment 3:
Building Process

6. What precautions should be taken to prevent static electricity damage during the building process?

7. When is the appropriate time to connect peripherals like the monitor, keyboard, and mouse during the building process?

Assignment 4:
BIOS Configuration and OS Installation

8. How do you access the BIOS/UEFI firmware, and what settings can be configured in this environment?

9. What methods can be used to install the operating system (OS) on a newly built computer system?

Assignment 5:
Troubleshooting and Performance Optimization

10. What steps can be taken to troubleshoot boot issues in a newly assembled computer system?

11. Why is it crucial to verify hardware compatibility, especially concerning the motherboard and CPU?

12. How can monitoring tools help optimize system performance, and what parameters do they track?

Assignment 6:
Temperature Management and System Maintenance

13. Why is evaluating the case's airflow important, and what adjustments can be made if necessary?

14. What additional cooling solutions can be considered for temperature optimization?

15. What practices contribute to effective dust management in a computer system?

Assignment 7:
Reflection on System Maintenance Practices

16. Explain the significance of implementing a regular backup strategy for system maintenance.

17. Why is it crucial to install and update antivirus and anti-malware software for system security?

18. Discuss the importance of keeping the OS, drivers, and software up to date in a computer system.

Created By Writer Hambirrao Sarnobat